READINGS FROM
PYTHON
FUNDAMENTALS

 CENGAGE

Australia • Brazil • Mexico • Singapore • United Kingdom • United States

CENGAGE

Readings from Python Fundamentals,
First Edition

SVP, Higher Education Product Management:
Erin Joyner

VP, Product Management: Thais Alencar

Product Team Manager: Kristin McNary

Product Assistant: Tom Benedetto

Director, Learning Design: Rebecca von Gillern

Senior Manager, Learning Design: Leigh Hefferon

Learning Designer: Mary Convertino

Vice President, Marketing – Science,
Technology, & Math: Jason Sakos

Senior Marketing Director: Michele McTighe

Marketing Manager: Cassie Cloutier

Senior Marketing Development Manager:
Samantha Best

Director, Content Creation: Juliet Steiner

Senior Manager, Content Creation: Patty Stephan

Senior Content Manager:
Michelle Ruelos Cannistraci

Director, Digital Production Services:
Krista Kellman

Production Service/Composition: SPi Global

Design Director: Jack Pendleton

Designer: Erin Griffin

Text Designer: Erin Griffin

Cover Designer: Erin Griffin

Cover image: ESB

For product information and technology assistance, contact us at
Cengage Customer & Sales Support, 1-800-354-9706
or support.cengage.com.

For permission to use material from this text or product, submit all requests online at **www.cengage.com/permissions.**

Library of Congress Control Number: 2020905203

ISBN: 978-0-357-63644-2

Cengage
200 Pier 4 Boulevard
Boston, MA 02210
USA

Cengage is a leading provider of customized learning solutions with employees residing in nearly 40 different countries and sales in more than 125 countries around the world. Find your local representative at **www.cengage.com**.

Cengage products are represented in Canada by
Nelson Education, Ltd.

To learn more about Cengage platforms and services, register or access your online learning solution, or purchase materials for your course, visit **www.cengage.com**.

Notice to the Reader

Publisher does not warrant or guarantee any of the products described herein or perform any independent analysis in connection with any of the product information contained herein. Publisher does not assume, and expressly disclaims, any obligation to obtain and include information other than that provided to it by the manufacturer. The reader is expressly warned to consider and adopt all safety precautions that might be indicated by the activities described herein and to avoid all potential hazards. By following the instructions contained herein, the reader willingly assumes all risks in connection with such instructions. The publisher makes no representations or warranties of any kind, including but not limited to, the warranties of fitness for particular purpose or merchantability, nor are any such representations implied with respect to the material set forth herein, and the publisher takes no responsibility with respect to such material. The publisher shall not be liable for any special, consequential, or exemplary damages resulting, in whole or part, from the readers' use of, or reliance upon, this material.

Printed in the USA
1 2 3 4 5   28 27 26 25 24

BRIEF CONTENTS

TABLE OF CONTENTS

Welcome to *Readings from Python Fundamentals*. This text includes the stand-alone lessons and readings from MindTap for *Python Fundamentals* and is intended to be used in conjunction with the full MindTap digital course for a complete learning experience.

- Write encapsulated and succinct Python functions
- Build Python classes using object-oriented programming
- Manipulate files on the filesystem (i.e., open, read, write, and delete)

MINDTAP COURSE OVERVIEW

Welcome to the Python Fundamentals MindTap Course! This text is organized into 9 modules. As you work with the language, you'll learn about control statements, delve into controlling program flow, and gradually work on more structured programs via functions. This MindTap teaches problem-solving skills for building efficient applications. As you settle into the Python ecosystem, you'll learn about data structures and study ways to correctly store and represent information. By working through specific examples, you'll learn how Python implements object-oriented programming (OOP) concepts of abstraction, encapsulation of data, inheritance, and polymorphism. Coverage also includes an overview of how imports, modules, and packages work in Python, how you can handle errors to prevent apps from crashing, as well as file manipulation.

Course Objectives:

- Use control statements
- Manipulate primitive and non-primitive data structures
- Use loops to iterate over objects or data for accurate results

MINDTAP COURSE FEATURES

In addition to the readings included within this text, the MindTap course includes the following:

Practice Exercises: Ungraded practice labs presented in an IDE provide an opportunity to practice a new concept in a short coding activity. Students are provided with guided instructional materials alongside a live computing environment.

Coding Snippets: These short, ungraded coding activities are embedded within the MindTap Reader and provide students an opportunity to practice new programming concepts "in-the-moment."

Lab Activities: Graded coding activities that are completed by a student and contain auto-grading feeds directly to the gradebook. Learners demonstrate an understanding of numerous concepts by completing tasks. Tasks are verified using unit tests, I/O tests, image and webpage comparison, debugging tests, and many other checks.

Module Lab Assessments: At the completion of a module, students are asked to complete a larger, authentic assignment with many tasks that encompasses the learning objectives covered throughout the module. These assessments are partially automatically graded and partially manually graded. Some tasks will be verified using unit tests, I/O tests, image and webpage comparison, and debugging tests but other tasks will be unique to each student's project and will require manual grading.

Capstone Lab Assessment: Provides a similar experience but occurs at the end of the course and incorporates objectives presented throughout the entirety of the course's modules. The goal of these lab assessments is to prove that students have mastered the learning objectives in the module and/or greater course, and in doing so have also created programs for their GitHub portfolio.

Module Quizzes: A short multiple-choice quiz at the end of each module encourages students to check their understanding before moving on to the next lesson.

Module Exam: Includes a total of over 450 multiple-choice Test Bank Questions to create tests and evaluate student mastery of each module.

PowerPoint: Students can use the PowerPoints to review key concepts.

Note: Within this text, some coding figures appear to be omitted or skipped. These coding figures only appear in the online lab environment and thus do not appear in the text.

INTRODUCING PYTHON

MODULE OBJECTIVES

BY THE END OF THIS MODULE, YOU WILL BE ABLE TO:

1. Use the Python interactive shell to write simple programs
2. Write and run simple Python scripts
3. Write and run dynamic scripts that take arguments from the command line
4. Use variables and describe the different types of values that variables can be assigned
5. Get user input from the keyboard for your Python programs
6. Explain the importance of comments and write them in Python
7. Explain the importance of whitespace and indentation in Python

INTRODUCTION

This module introduces the Python programming language. We will work with the Python interpreter and write our first Python program.

Python is a high-level, general-purpose programming language. It is notorious for having a very simple "pseudo-code-like" syntax that places emphasis on readability and expressiveness. This not only makes code simpler to write but also easier to maintain. Additionally, it features a vast standard library that is augmented by an even larger array of third-party libraries. These are all developed and supported by Python's very active community.

Development is also faster in Python, as it is an interpreted language. This means that the instructions are interpreted at runtime and there's no need to pre-compile the program into machine language instructions. This makes for quick prototyping and experimentation. Python's interpreted nature, along with its dynamic typing system, are what really set it apart from languages such as Java or C++.

Python also supports multiple paradigms, such as the following:

- Object-oriented programming
- Functional programming
- Imperative programming
- Procedural programming

This versatility, coupled with Python's ability to run on all operating system platforms from Windows and GNU/Linux to macOS, have led to its popularity. As a matter of fact, today, Python comes built into most GNU/Linux distributions as well as macOS.

Python can be applied for writing automation scripts, machine learning, scientific computation, big data, web applications, GUI programming, IoT devices—just about anything. It's a multipurpose language and is easy to extend. Because of this, Python has been adopted by tech companies such as Google (for YouTube), Uber, Facebook, and Mozilla, further ensuring its support and development.

In this chapter, we will write our first Python program and play with the interpreter through the use of the Python interactive shell. We will also take a look at the different ways of running a Python program.

Python 2 Versus Python 3

Before we move on to getting our hands dirty, we will take a brief look at the history of Python. Out there in the wild, you'll find codebases that use Python 3 or the older Python 2. The two are very similar. Generally, a lot of the code written for Python 3 will run on Python 2 and vice versa, but this should not be depended on as there are a few syntactic differences that can bring about issues. However, the majority of the differences between the two are under the hood.

Currently, support still runs for Python 2, but Python 3 is the only one in active development, meaning any new features brought to the language are only developed for Python 3. Additionally, the majority of commonly used third-party libraries have now ported to Python 3 and are withdrawing development for their Python 2 versions. For this reason, we will be using Python 3.7 for all of the examples in this course.

LESSON 1.1 WORKING WITH THE PYTHON INTERACTIVE SHELL

We are going to be writing our first program through the Python interactive shell. Before we begin, ensure that you have Python installed on your machine. We can check this by opening the Python interpreter. To open the interpreter, enter the `python` command at the command line.

> Practice this concept by completing Practice Exercise 1.1A: Checking our Python Installation.

After the interactive shell opens, as shown in **Figure 1.1**, on the first line, you should see the Python version information. This includes its major version and the release date. As you can see from the preceding screenshot, it shows us that we're using Python 3, minor version 7, which was released on December 23, 2018. We can also see information on the system the interactive shell is running on. On the second line, we can see a few examples of commands we can write, and finally the prompt to enter a command >>> on the third line.

The Python interactive shell can be thought of as just any other shell that interfaces with the operating system (for example, Bash or CMD), but in this case, it interfaces with the Python interpreter. Through it, we can execute Python instructions. It presents a command-line interface. You can enter commands directly in the command line for execution.

> Practice this concept by completing Practice Exercise 1.1B: Working with the Python Interpreter.

When you exit the Python interactive shell and relaunch it, you will notice that any variables you had defined or commands you had run in the previous session are gone. Therefore, we can't reuse them.

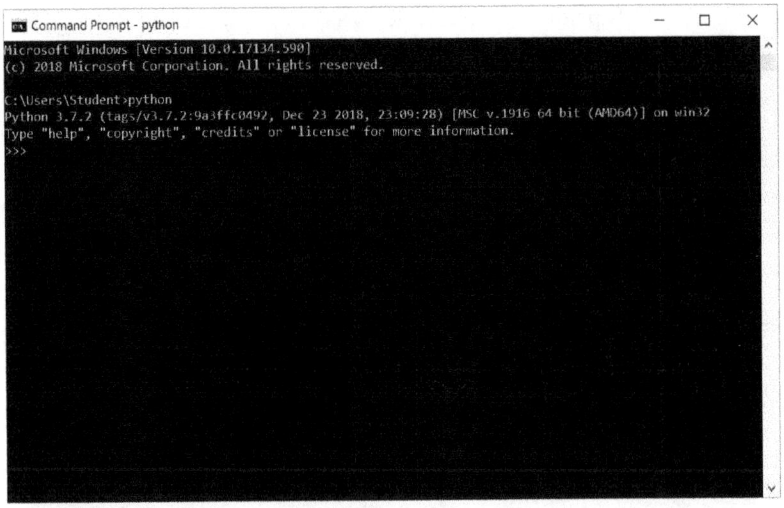

Figure 1.1   Checking the Python installation

In addition to entering commands directly in the command line, another way to run a Python program is by running code that has been saved in a file. This allows us to run many instructions at a time and also reuse them, as we will see later on in the course. In the next lesson, we will take a look at how to do this.

Test yourself on this concept by completing Lab Activity 1.1: Working with the Python Shell.

LESSON 1.2 WRITING AND RUNNING SIMPLE SCRIPTS

Running quick commands through the interactive shell is fun. It comes in handy when you have a quick hypothesis that you want to test out or when you want to check whether a specific method exists for some data type. However, you can't really write a full-fledged program through the interactive shell.

Python allows you to run your instructions from a saved file. A file containing Python instructions is called a **module**. A script is a module that can be run. Anything you can run on the interactive shell can be written and run as a Python script.

By convention, Python scripts should have the file extension .py. The filename should be a valid filename, as defined by your operating system.

Practice this concept by completing Practice Exercise 1.2: Creating a Script.

Assume you have file test1.py containing the code shown in **Snippet 1.6**.

Snippet 1.6

```
print("---------------------------------")
print("Hello " * 5)
print("---------------------------------")
```

When you run the command python test1.py at the command line, python opens the file and executes each instruction, line by line. First, it runs the call to print on the first line and prints out a series of dashes.

It then calls the second `print`, which prints the message five times, hence the `* 5` bit. This can be any value you want and is basically a shorthand way of saying, "repeat that string of characters an *n* number of times", *n* being 5 in our case. For example, if you change that 5 to `100`, it will print `Hello` 100 times, as shown in **Snippet 1.7**.

Snippet 1.7

```
print("-------------------------------------")
print("Hello " * 100)
print("-------------------------------------")
```

The output is shown in **Figure 1.3**.

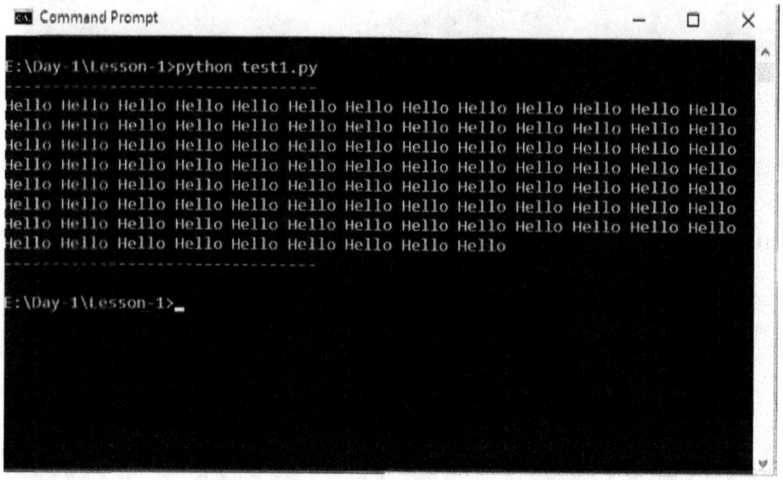

Figure 1.3   Creating and running the script with modified values

Finally, the last line is executed, just like our first, and prints out dashes. This execution is done in a blocking manner, so each line is executed after the previous line has completed running.

Lesson 1.2.1 Running a File Containing Invalid Commands

As with the interactive shell, putting in invalid instructions also causes an error. Assume you modify `test1.py` from Lesson 1.2 to match **Snippet 1.8** and try to run it:

Snippet 1.8

```
print("-------------------------------------")
print(invalid instruction)
print("-------------------------------------")
```

You should see an error as shown in **Figure 1.4**. This output is called a **stack trace**. It tells us useful things such as where the error happened, what kind of error it was, and what other calls were triggered along the way when we ran our command. Stack traces should be read from bottom to top. Another name for a stack trace is a **traceback**.

The last line tells us what kind of error was raised, that is, a `SyntaxError`, meaning that our instructions were invalid. The line above it logs out the source line that caused the error, and the first line references our `test1.py` module where the line is located. You will be seeing different types of errors as you go through this course, and there will be an in-depth look at errors and exception handling in one of the later modules. For now, it is important that you understand how to read a stack trace and identify what is causing the error, and then act accordingly to fix it.

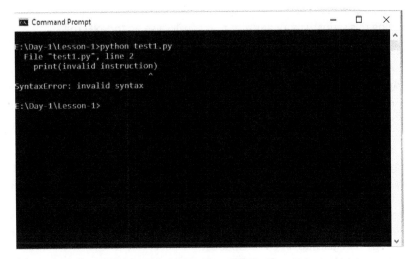

Figure 1.4   Running the file with invalid syntax

PASSING USER ARGUMENTS TO SCRIPTS

To make a script more dynamic, you can have the user provide arguments to it when calling it.

Assume you have a file named `test2.py` that contains the code shown in **Snippet 1.9**.

Snippet 1.9

```
import sys

print("This argument was passed to the script:", sys.argv[1])
```

You would run the script as usual, passing it an argument, as illustrated in **Snippet 1.10**.

Snippet 1.10

```
python test2.py foobar
```

The output is shown in **Figure 1.5**.

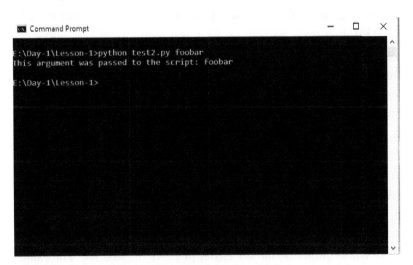

Figure 1.5   Passing arguments to the script

NOTE Running this script without any arguments will raise an **IndexError**.

We have some new syntax in this script. We won't go over all of it in detail in this chapter, but for the purposes of this explanation, `import sys` imports the `sys` module that is built into Python into our script. This module provides access to Python interpreter functions. It is being used here to read command-line arguments that have been passed to the interpreter when invoking our script.

When we call `sys.argv[1]`, we are asking for the first argument that's been passed when running the script. Generally, you can pass as many arguments as you like by separating each argument with a blank space.

 NOTE If you want to pass an argument that contains spaces, enclose it in quotes. For example, `python test2.py "argument with a space"`.

Test yourself on this concept by completing Lab Activity 1.2: Running Simply Python Scripts.

LESSON 1.3 PYTHON SYNTAX

In this lesson, we will see how the Python language expressions are structured. Essentially, we will learn what it takes to write a valid Python program.

Lesson 1.3.1 Variables

As we know, variables are references to values in memory.

Variables in Python can reference values of different data types such as strings, integers, floating point values, Booleans, and different data types and data structures, as we will see later on in this course. Python, in contrast to statically typed languages such as Java or C++, doesn't require you to pre-declare a variable's data type. It determines the type during runtime.

You can think of a variable as a box with a named label on it. The box on its own has no value but becomes valuable after you put something inside it. The box represents the things inside it and, similarly, a variable is used to represent the value inside it.

Additionally, a variable's value and type can change during runtime. Any variable can be used to store any data type and can be used as long as it has already been defined. Before we look at how to assign variables to values, let's briefly go over the different types of values/data types that have been encountered thus far and the ones we will be dealing with in this chapter.

VALUES

Python supports several different types of values. These values are what variables can be assigned to. Thus far, we have encountered strings and numeric values such as integers.

NUMERIC VALUES—INTEGERS

Mathematically, integers are whole numbers that are either positive or negative. The same definition is applicable for Python integers.

Here is an example of an integer expression in Python. As we saw earlier, Python echoes whatever you write in the interactive shell as shown in **Snippet 1.11**.

Snippet 1.11

```
>>> 7
7
>>>
```

We also saw the different symbols, such as +, *, and -, that can be used to perform different arithmetic operations on the integer values as shown in **Snippet 1.12**.

Snippet 1.12

```
>>> 5 + 4 + 6 + 9
24
>>> 5 * 5
25
>>> 42 - 16
26
>>>
```

We can also check the type of a value by using the `type` function that is built into Python.

Practice this concept by completing Practice Exercise 1.3A: Checking the Type of a Value.

 NOTE   The part in the output before `int` says `class` because everything in Python is an object.

There are a few other numeric types of values, such as floating-point numbers, but we will review those in the next module.

STRING VALUES

Another type of value that we have seen in Practice Exercise 1.3A was a string value. This is a sequence of characters that's placed in between two quotation marks, for example, `"January"`, `"Chops Maloy"`, and `'UB40'`. You can use both double and single quotes to denote strings. Strings can contain numbers, letters, and symbols as shown in **Snippet 1.17**.

Snippet 1.17

```
>>> type("3 Musketeers")
<class 'str'>
>>> type('First Order!')
<class 'str'>
>>>
```

As you can see from Snippet 1.17, it tells us that the type of the value `"3 Musketeers"` is `str` (short for string).

TYPE CONVERSION

Sometimes, you may have a string with an integer inside it or an integer that you want to put in a string. The first scenario often happens with user input in which everything is returned inside a string. To be able to use it, we need to convert it to the desired data type.

Python allows you to convert string type values to integer type values and vice versa. Using the built-in `str` function, you can convert an integer to a string as shown in **Snippet 1.18**.

Snippet 1.18

```
>>> str(7)
'7'
>>>
```

Strings can also be converted to integers, as long as they hold a valid integer value within. This is done by use of the built-in `int` function as shown in **Snippet 1.19**.

Snippet 1.19

```
>>> int("100")
100
>>>
```

An error occurs if we try converting a string that doesn't contain an integer. In **Snippet 1.20**, the string `"Foobar"` can't be converted because it is a string of letters. `"3.14159"` also fails because it is a float, and not an integer.

Snippet 1.20

```
>>> int("Foobar")
Traceback (most recent call last):
  File "<stdin>", line 1, in <module>
ValueError: invalid literal for int() with base 10: 'Foobar'
>>> int("3.14159")
Traceback (most recent call last):
  File "<stdin>", line 1, in <module>
ValueError: invalid literal for int() with base 10: '3.14159'
>>>
```

These are the basic types of values we will be dealing with in this module.

ASSIGNING VARIABLES

You assign a value to a variable in Python using the syntax shown in **Snippet 1.21**.

Snippet 1.21

```
>>> number = 7
>>>
```

Printing the variable to the standard output will reveal its value as shown in **Snippet 1.22**.

Snippet 1.22

```
>>> print(number)
7
>>>
```

However, if we try using a variable before assigning it a value, the Python interpreter will raise an error. Consider the code in **Snippet 1.23**.

Snippet 1.23

```
>>> del number
>>> print(number)
Traceback (most recent call last):
  File "<stdin>", line 1, in <module>
NameError: name 'number' is not defined
>>>
```

On the first line, we are using a new statement: `del`. `del` unbinds a name/variable (Python refers to variables as names) from the current namespace. Calling `del number` thus deletes the variable `number` from the current namespace.

 NOTE   A namespace is a mapping of names/variables to their values.

This means that the reference `number` is removed and no longer points to the value 7. When we try printing out the now nonexistent variable, we get an error stating that the name `number` is not defined.

We use variables when we have a value in our code that we want to use multiple times. They prevent us from having to repeat that value each time we want to use it, as variables store the values in memory.

When we store values in memory, we can reuse them as many times as we would like.

Practice this concept by completing Practice Exercise 1.3B: Using Variables.

Consider the statements shown in **Snippet 1.34**.

Snippet 1.34

```
>>> message = "I love Python"
>>> message + "!" * 3
'I love Python!!!'
>>>
```

In Snippet 1.34 we can see the application of a new operation to strings: +. We use this whenever we want to concatenate (add together) two strings.

This only applies to strings, and thus trying to concatenate a string with any other data type will raise an error. We will study this in greater depth in the next chapter.

An interesting phenomenon with Python variables is that they are not deeply linked as demonstrated in **Snippet 1.35**.

Snippet 1.35

```
>>> x = 1
>>> y = x
>>> x = 2
>>> print(x)
2
>>> print(y)
1
>>>
```

A behavior you'd expect would be that y being assigned to x would change upon changing x, but it doesn't; it stays the same. What do you think is happening?

Because Python variables point to values in memory, when y is assigned to x, it does not make an alias for x but instead points the variable y to where the value of x, 1, is. Changing x changes its pointer from 1 to 2, but y remains pointing to its initial value as illustrated in **Figure 1.7**.

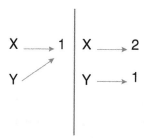

Figure 1.7   Variable assignment

MULTIPLE ASSIGNMENT

In Python, you can also assign multiple variables in one statement, as shown in **Snippet 1.36**.

Snippet 1.36

```
>>> a, b, c = 1, 2, 3
>>> print(a)
1
>>> print(b)
2
>>> print(c)
3
>>>
```

The assignment works so that the first variable, a, is assigned the first value, 1, after the = sign. The second variable, b, is assigned the second value, 2, and the third variable, c, is assigned the third value, 3.

What happens if we try to assign more variables than we pass values, as shown in **Snippet 1.37**?

Snippet 1.37

```
>>> a, b, c = 1, 2
Traceback (most recent call last):
  File "<stdin>", line 1, in <module>
ValueError: not enough values to unpack (expected 3, got 2)
>>>
```

The Python interpreter raises an error and states that it didn't get enough values to assign to the variables we declared in our statement.

A similar error is raised when we try to assign more values than there are variables as shown in **Snippet 1.38**.

Snippet 1.38

```
>>> a, b = 1, 2, 3
Traceback (most recent call last):
  File "<stdin>", line 1, in <module>
ValueError: too many values to unpack (expected 2)
>>>
```

Test yourself on this concept by completing Lab Activity 1.3A: Using Variables and Assign Statements.

So far, we have learned how variables are used in Python and a few of the different values you can assign to them. We have also learned how to use variables in our programs. In the next section, we will be looking at the rules for naming variables.

NAMING IDENTIFIERS AND RESERVED WORDS

Python, like other languages, has a couple of rules on naming identifiers such as variable names, class names, function names, module names, and other objects. Some are strictly enforced by the interpreter, while others are simply enforced by convention, and developers are at liberty to ignore them. The rules and conventions are designed to avoid confusion when the interpreter is parsing through code or to make the code more easily readable by humans.

We start off by going through some of the rules for naming variables and other identifiers:

- An identifier can consist of upper and lowercase letters of the alphabet, underscores, unicode identifiers, and digits 0 to 9.
- An identifier cannot begin with a digit; for example, 7x is an invalid variable name.
- No other characters can be in identifiers. This includes spaces or any other symbols. Spaces most notably occur in module names as some operating systems will permit filenames with spaces. This should be avoided.
- A Python keyword cannot be used in an identifier name, for example, import, if, for, and lambda.

Snippet 1.39 shows examples of valid variable definitions.

Snippet 1.39

```
>>> meaning_of_life = 42
>>> COUNTRY = "Wakanda"
>>> Ω = 38.12
>>> myDiv = "<div></div>"
>>> letter6 = "f"
>>>
```

It should also be noted that Python identifier names are case sensitive. Consider the statement in **Snippet 1.40**.

Snippet 1.40

```
>>> foobar = 5
```

The variable shown in Snippet 1.40 is a different variable from the one shown in **Snippet 1.41**.

Snippet 1.41

```
>>> Foobar = 5
```

Certain names in Python cannot be used as they are parts of the language syntax. Such words are known as **reserved words** or **keywords**. An example of a reserved word is import, which is a statement used for when you want to import a module into your code.

Python has several keywords. You can use Python's help utility to see a list of keywords.

Practice this concept by completing Practice Exercise 1.3C: Python Keywords.

You should not use any word from the list of keywords as an identifier name. Note that you don't have to remember them all as the Python interpreter will restrict you from using them.

In the example shown in **Snippet 1.45**, we are trying to use the keyword for, but we get a syntax error upon doing so. The same applies for all keywords.

Snippet 1.45

```
>>> for = "Elise"
  File "<stdin>", line 1
    for = "Elise"
        ^
SyntaxError: invalid syntax
>>>
```

PYTHON NAMING CONVENTIONS

Python has several guidelines for naming identifiers that aren't enforced by the interpreter. These guidelines are meant for consistent code and making it more readable. Please note that these are simply guidelines and the programmer is at liberty to ignore them.

It should be counterpointed that ignoring naming conventions eventually leads to a road of regret as they provide several advantages, such as the following:

- Makes the code easier to read and understand for other programmers, because they would find consistent and instantly recognizable patterns
- Enhances clarity and reduces ambiguity
- Makes automated refactoring easier, as the automation tools would have consistent patterns to look for
- Provides additional information about the identifiers; for example, when you see a variable name in all caps, you immediately know that it is a constant

Some of these conventions and guidelines are given here. Compound variable names should be written in snake_case notation. It is better to use the name shown in **Snippet 1.46** rather than the ones shown in **Snippet 1.47**.

Snippet 1.46

```
>>> first_letter = "a"
```

Snippet 1.47

```
>>> firstLetter = "a"    # camelCase
>>> FirstLetter = "a"    # PascalCase
```

Naming for constants should be written in capital letters to denote that their values are not meant to change, as shown in **Snippet 1.48**. In reality, though, Python has no way of restricting the value of a constant from being changed as they are variables, just like any other.

Snippet 1.48

```
>>> NUMBER_OF_PLANETS = 8
>>> RADIUS_OF_THE_EARTH_IN_KM = 6371
```

Note that we can change a constant's value as shown in **Snippet 1.49**.

Snippet 1.49

```
>>> NUMBER_OF_PLANETS = 9
>>>
```

Avoid lowercase l or uppercase O as single character variable names, as in some fonts, these letters can be mistaken for 1 and 0, respectively, making the code harder to read.

In the next lesson, we will learn about comments, their importance, and how to write them in Python.

Test yourself on this concept by completing Lab Activity 1.3B: Variable Assignment and Variable Naming Conventions.

LESSON 1.4 USER INPUT, COMMENTS, AND INDENTATIONS

In this lesson, we will look at how to take user input from the keyboard, how to write comments, and the importance of indentation while writing Python code.

USER INPUT FROM THE KEYBOARD

Python has a very handy function for obtaining user keyboard input from the command line interface CLI called `input()`. When called, this function allows the user to type input into the program using the keyboard. The execution of the program pauses until the user presses the **Enter** key after completing the input. The user's input is then passed to your program as a string that you can use. The following is an example of this:

Declare the variable shown in **Snippet 1.50**.

Snippet 1.50

```
>>> message = input()
```

The program execution will halt until you input a value and hit the **Enter** key. **Snippet 1.51** shows a value entered.

Snippet 1.51

```
Peter Piper picked a peck of pickled peppers
>>>
```

The `message` variable was assigned to the value that we passed in Snippet 1.51. Let's print it out as shown in **Snippet 1.52**.

Snippet 1.52

```
>>> print(message)
Peter Piper picked a peck of pickled peppers
>>>
```

PASSING IN A PROMPT TO THE INPUT FUNCTION

You may have noted that there is no cue that lets us know when to type or what to type. You can pass a prompt to the `input` function to do this. The prompt is written to standard output without a trailing newline and serves as a cue for the user to pass in the input. Let's view this in action.

Declare the variable shown in **Snippet 1.53**, passing in the prompt `Enter a tongue twister:` to the `input` function. This will be displayed to the user.

Snippet 1.53

```
>>> tongue_twister = input("Enter a tongue twister: ")
Enter a tongue twister:
```

Let's type in our tongue twister and hit the **Enter** key. The `tongue_twister` variable will then be set, and printing it out should reveal the value we passed as shown in **Snippet 1.54**.

Snippet 1.54

```
Enter a tongue twister: She sells seashells by the seashore
>>> print(tongue_twister)
She sells seashells by the seashore
>>>
```

USING DIFFERENT INPUT DATA TYPES IN YOUR PROGRAM

The values returned by the `input` function are always strings. Sometimes, a string may not be the data type you are expecting in your program. As we saw earlier, you can convert strings to integers using the built-in `int` function. To retrieve integer values from user input, all your program needs to do is cast the string that is returned as a value by the `input` function. **Snippet 1.55** shows an example of this.

Snippet 1.55

```
>>> number = int(input("Find the square root of: "))
Find the square root of: 49
>>> print("The square root of", number, "is", number ** 0.5 )
The square root of 49 is 7.0
```

In **Snippet 1.55**, we take the user's input which is a string, convert it to an integer using the `int` function, and print out its square root.

Practice this concept by completing Practice Exercise 1.4A: Fetching and Using User Input.

We can get user input to use in our program in Python by using the built-in `input` function. You can pass a prompt argument to the `input` function that will act as a cue for the user to pass the input. The `input` function always returns values as strings that we can optionally cast to the data type we desire.

COMMENTS

Comments are an integral part of programming.

Comments can be thought of as notes on the code that give more contextual information about it. They can explain why certain decisions were made, some improvements that can be made in future, and also note the business logic. In short, they make the code easier to understand for humans.

There are three different ways to write Python comments, **documentation strings_(docstrings** for short), inline comments, and block comments.

BLOCK AND INLINE COMMENTS

Block and inline comments start with a pound sign, #. A **block comment** comes in the line before the statement it annotates and is placed at the same indentation level as shown in **Snippet 1.59**.

Snippet 1.59

```
# increment counter
counter = counter + 1
```

Inline comments are placed on the same line as the statement it annotates as shown in **Snippet 1.60**.

Snippet 1.60

```
>>> print(foobar)   # this will raise an error because foobar isn't defined
```

Block comments are applied to the code that follows them and should be indented at the same level as the code it is meant for. Although they serve the same purpose as inline comments, block comments are to be preferred by convention as they are more immediately noticeable and unambiguous as to the code they are annotating.

DOCUMENTATION STRINGS

A documentation string, or docstring for short, is a literal string used as a Python comment. It is written and wrapped within triple quotation marks: """ or '''. Docstrings are often used to document modules, functions, and class definitions. The following is an example module that has been documented with a docstring. Module docstrings should be put at the beginning of the file. **Snippet 1.61** shows an example.

Snippet 1.61

```
"""
This script can be called with two integer arguments to return their sum
"""
import sys
num_1 = int(sys.argv[1])
num_2 = int(sys.argv[2])

print(num_1, "+", num_2, "=", num_1 + num_2)
```

Furthermore, you can also use docstrings to write multiline comments as shown in **Snippet 1.62**.

Snippet 1.62

```
"""
This loop goes through all the numbers from 1 to 100 printing each
out
"""
for i in range(1, 101):
  print(i)
```

Sufficiently commenting your code leads to easily maintainable and easier-to-read code. Because we often spend more time reading code than writing it, it is important that we write comments, but even more important is that we write code clearly enough to need as few explanations as possible.

INDENTATION

A **block** is a group of statements that are meant to be executed together. Blocks are a fundamental aspect of modern programming languages because flow-of-control structures (structures that determine the flow of execution of code) are formed from blocks. Blocks allow a set of statements to be executed as though they were a single statement. Different languages represent blocks differently, but most commonly, the syntax shown in **Snippet 1.63** is used.

Snippet 1.63

```
if (true) {
    // execute this block of statements
} else {
    // execute other block of statements
}
```

 NOTE   `if` is a common control flow structure that evaluates Boolean expressions and determines where the program should go.

In the preceding code snippet, a block is denoted by whatever is inside the curly braces. If the condition is true, then execute a certain block of statements; otherwise, execute the other block. Often, blocks can be nested within other blocks.

In Python, statements are grouped using whitespace, that is, blocks are indented within other blocks instead of using curly braces.

NOTE   Whitespace is any character in a piece of text that occupies space but doesn't correspond to a visible marking.

Observe the code in **Snippet 1.64**, which is the Python equivalent of Snippet 1.63.

Snippet 1.64

```
if True:
    # execute this block of statements
    print("Block 1")
else:
    # execute other block of statements
    print("Block 2")
```

Python uses whitespace to denote blocks. Just as blocks are denoted by statements enclosed in curly braces in several other languages, any statement that is indented in Python forms a new block, becoming a child of the previous statement with the parent statement being suffixed with a colon, `:` In place of a closing curly brace, a statement that would come after that block would be outdented outside it, as shown with the `else` statement that came after the `if` block.

Generally, you can use any number of spaces as long as every statement in the block has an equal amount of indentation, although the standard is four spaces. An example is shown in **Snippet 1.65**.

Snippet 1.65

```
if True:
    x = 5
    y = x
    print(x, y ** 2)
```

If we try running a piece of code without proper indentation, Python will raise an error.

Practice this concept by completing Practice Exercise 1.4B: The Importance of Proper Indentation.

Test yourself on this concept by completing Lab Activity 1.4A: Fixing Indentations in a Code Block.

 NOTE   Although you can use any number of spaces to indent a statement, the general convention is to use four spaces.

Test yourself on this concept by completing Lab Activity 1.4B: Implementing User Input and Comments in a Script.

SUMMARY

In this module, we have looked at two ways of running Python programs. We can run commands through the Python interactive shell or by running saved scripts. While you will mostly find yourself running programs from saved scripts, you will find the freedom and quick gratification of using the interactive shell to run a quick check very convenient. These two methods will come in handy on your Python journey.

We have also covered the Python syntax in detail in this module. We started with variable assignment in Python and then looked at the different types of values Python variables can be assigned to, the syntax for assigning them, as well as the importance of reserved keywords in Python.

We then looked at the built-in `input` function and how it enables us to take input from a user keyboard. We looked at the different ways of writing comments in Python code, and then finished the module by looking at the importance of indentation in writing readable, maintainable Python code.

In the next module, we will look at data types such as integers, strings, Booleans, and more.

DATA TYPES

MODULE OBJECTIVES

BY THE END OF THIS MODULE, YOU WILL BE ABLE TO:

1. Explain the different numerical data types
2. Use operators on numerical data types
3. Explain strings and implement string operations, such as indexing, slicing, and string formatting
4. Describe escape sequences
5. Explain lists and perform simple operations on them
6. Use Boolean expressions and Boolean operators

INTRODUCTION

This module introduces the data types available to us. We look at integers, strings, lists, and Booleans.

In Module 1, we learned about variables and looked at a few of the values/types of data that can be assigned to them. Specifically, we dealt with data of the string and integer types. In this module, we will look at the other data types that Python supports. Data types classify data, to tell the interpreter how the program intends to utilize that data. Data types define the different operations that can be performed on the data, how the data is stored, and the meaning of the data.

LESSON 2.1 NUMERICAL DATA

Let's begin with numerical data types.

Lesson 2.1.1 Types of Numbers

INTEGERS

Integers, as we saw in Module 1 - Introducing Python, are numerical data types that are comprised of whole numbers. Whole numbers can be either negative or positive. In **Snippet 2.1**, we will see how Python represents integers, and then we can check their types.

Snippet 2.1

```
>>> integer = 49
>>> negative_integer = -35
>>> print(type(integer), integer)
<class 'int'> 49
>>> print(type(negative_integer), negative_integer)
<class 'int'> -35
>>>
```

Additionally, Python integers have unlimited precision. This means that there are no limits to how large they can be (save for the amount of available memory), as shown in **Snippet 2.2**.

Snippet 2.2

```
>>> large_integer =
34567898327463893216847532149022563647754227885439016662145553364327889985421
>>> print(large_integer)
34567898327463893216847532149022563647754227885439016662145553364327889985421
>>>
```

FLOATING POINT NUMBERS

Another numerical type supported by Python is floating point numbers. The type for this kind of value is `float`. As we saw in Module 1, these are represented as shown in **Snippet 2.3**.

Snippet 2.3

```
>>> n = 3.3333
>>> print(n)
3.3333
>>> import math
>>> print(type(math.pi), math.pi)
<class 'float'>, 3.141592653589793
>>> print(type(math.e), math.e)
<class 'float'>, 2.718281828459045
>>>
```

Here, we import `math`, which is a built-in Python library that provides access to different mathematical functions and constants. We print out the type and the values of the constants Pi (`math.pi`) and Euler's number (`math.e`). The displayed values are approximated.

Furthermore, you can convert an integer to a floating point value by using the `float` function as shown in **Snippet 2.4**.

Snippet 2.4

```
>>> float(23)
23.0
>>>
```

BINARY, HEXADECIMAL, AND OCTAL NUMBERS

Binary, hexadecimal, and octal numbers are alternative number systems, as opposed to the common decimal number system that we are accustomed to. Binary numbers are numbers expressed in the *base 2* system, which uses only 0s and 1s to represent numbers.

To write binary numbers in Python, write the number and prefix it with 0b. Typing a binary number on the interactive shell outputs its decimal equivalent as shown in **Snippet 2.5**.

Snippet 2.5

```
>>> 0b111
7
>>> 0b10
2
>>> 0b1000
8
>>>
```

Hexadecimal numbers are numbers that are expressed in the *base 16* system. The symbols 0, 1, 2, 3, 4, 5, 6, 7, 8, 9, a, b, c, d, e, and f are used to represent hexadecimal numbers. Hexadecimal numbers should be prefixed with 0x. Typing a hexadecimal number in the interpreter outputs its decimal equivalent as shown in **Snippet 2.6**.

Snippet 2.6

```
>>> 0xf
15
>>> 0x9ac
2476
>>> 0xaf
175
>>>
```

Finally, we have octal numbers, which are numbers written in the *base 8* numbering system. This system uses the digits from 0 to 7 to represent numbers. In Python, they should be prefixed with 0o. Typing an octal number in the interpreter outputs its decimal equivalent as shown in **Snippet 2.7**.

Snippet 2.7

```
>>> 0o20
16
>>> 0o200
128
>>> 0o113
75
>>>
```

To convert any decimal (*base 10*) number to binary, hexadecimal, or octal numbers, you can use the built-in `bin`, `hex`, and `oct` Python functions, respectively, as shown in **Snippet 2.8**.

Snippet 2.8

```
>>> bin(7)
'0b111'
>>> hex(700)
'0x2bc'
>>> oct(70)
'0o106'
>>>
```

> Practice this concept by completing Practice Exercise 2.1: Converting between Different Types of Number Systems.

Besides these types, Python also has support for complex numbers, which comes in handy for scientific calculations that require them, such as Fourier transforms, among others. Python offers several different numeric types and provides a straightforward, intuitive process for converting between them.

Lesson 2.1.2 Operators

In this lesson, we will discuss the different operators that Python makes available to us.

ARITHMETIC OPERATORS

Arithmetic operators are mathematical functions that take numerical values and perform calculations on them.

Numerical data types are only as valuable as the operations that you can carry out on them. All of the Python numeric types support the operations shown in **Figure 2.2**.

Figure 2.2 Arithmetic operators

Operator	Result
$x + y$	Sum of x and y
$x - y$	Difference of x and y
$x * y$	Product of x and y
x / y	Quotient of x and y
$x // y$	Floored quotient of x and y
$x \% y$	Remainder of x and y
$-x$	x negated
$+x$	x unchanged
abs(x)	Absolute value or magnitude of x
int(x)	x converted to integer
float(x)	x converted to floating point
divmod(x, y)	Returns the pair ($x // y$, $x \% y$)
pow(x, y)	x to the power y
$x ** y$	x to the power y

We will be demonstrating by using decimal numbers, but these operators can work on operands of any numeric type. As you've already seen, you can add numbers, as shown in **Snippet 2.10**.

Snippet 2.10

```
>>> 5 + 8 + 7
20
>>>
```

You can also carry out subtraction as shown in **Snippet 2.11**.

Snippet 2.11

```
>>> 20 - 5
15
>>>
```

And, you can also perform multiplication as shown in **Snippet 2.12**.

Snippet 2.12

```
>>> 4 * 3
12
>>>
```

Finally, you can perform division. This is shown in **Snippet 2.13**.

Snippet 2.13

```
>>> 12 / 3
4.0
>>>
```

 NOTE   The division of two numbers, regardless of their value types in Python, will always yield a floating point number.

Floor division is different from classic division, in that it always yields a whole integer. It is a division of two numbers, but the value yielded has any fractional parts discarded. Floor division is also referred to as integer division. An example is shown in **Snippet 2.14**.

Snippet 2.14

```
>>> 13 // 2  # classic division would yield 6.5
6
>>>
```

The modulo operation finds the remainder after the division of one number by another as shown in **Snippet 2.15**.

Snippet 2.15

```
>>> 5 % 2
1
>>> 20 % 3
2
>>>
```

Finally, we have the **exponentiation** operation, which raises a number to a specified power as shown in **Snippet 2.16**.

Snippet 2.16

```
>>> 5 ** 3
125
>>> 10 ** 4
10000
>>>
```

The difference between this method of exponentiation and using the pow function is that the pow function allows you to pass in a third argument, a divisor, which can be used to find the remainder after dividing the result (the exponentiated value) and the divisor.

ASSIGNMENT OPERATORS

Aside from the = simple **assignment** operator, Python has other assignment operators. These are shorthand variations of simple operators, in that they not only do an arithmetic operation but also reassign the variable. The table shown in **Figure 2.3** lists the most common assignment operators.

Figure 2.3   Assignment operators

Operator	Example	Equivalent to
+=	$x+ =7$	$x = x + 7$
-=	$x- =7$	$x = x - 7$
*=	$x*=7$	$x = x*7$
/=	$x/=7$	$x = x/7$
%=	$x \% = 7$	$x = x \% 7$
**=	$x** = 7$	$x = x**7$
//=	$x// = 7$	$x = x // 7$

Snippet 2.17 is an example of these operators in action. x is initially assigned to 10. We add 1 and then reassign x to the result of that operation, 11.

Snippet 2.17

```
>>> x = 10
>>> x += 1
>>> print(x)
11
>>>
```

The code shown in Snippet 2.17 is equivalent to the code shown in **Snippet 2.18**.

Snippet 2.18

```
>>> x = 10
>>> x = x + 1
>>> print(x)
11
>>>
```

The same principle is applicable for all of the operators that are listed in Figure 2.3.

You can perform all arithmetic operations in Python. All operators can be applied to all numeric types. Python also provides assignment operators as a shorthand way of performing an operation and assignment in one statement.

Lesson 2.1.3 Order of Operations

The **order of operations** is the collection of rules about which procedures should be evaluated first when evaluating an expression.

In Python, the order in which operators are evaluated is just as it is mathematically: **PEMDAS**.

Parentheses have the highest precedence. Expressions inside parentheses are evaluated first:

Snippet 2.19

```
>>> (9 + 2) * 2
22
>>>
```

Next, the exponentiation operator is given the second highest precedence:

Snippet 2.20

```
>>> 2 ** 3 + 2
10
>>>
```

Multiplication and division (including floor division and the modulo operation) have the same precedence. Addition and subtraction come next:

Snippet 2.21

```
>>> 8 * 3 + 1
25
>>> 24 / 6 - 2
2
>>> 7 + 5 - 3
9
```

In cases where two operators have the same precedence (for example, addition and subtraction), statements are evaluated left to right:

Snippet 2.22

```
>>> 7 - 5 + 4
6
>>> 10 / 5 * 3
6.0
```

The exception to the preceding rule is with exponents, which are evaluated from the right-most value. In the example shown in **Snippet 2.23**, the evaluation is equivalent to 2^(3^2).

Snippet 2.23

```
>>> 2**3**2
512
```

Let's go over what we have learned in this lesson before moving ahead:

- Python supports different numeric types: integers, floating point numbers, and binary, hexadecimal, and octal numbers, to name but a few.
- Python also supports complex numbers.
- Multiple operators can be applied to these different types of numbers.
- Assignment operators carry out the operation and reassign the variable to the result.
- Arithmetic operators in Python follow the standard order of operations as in mathematics: PEMDAS.

Test yourself on this concept by completing Lab Activity 2.1A: Order of Operations.

Test yourself on this concept by completing Lab Activity 2.1B: Using Different Arithmetic Operators.

LESSON 2.2 STRINGS

In this lesson, we will look at strings in detail.

Lesson 2.2.1 String Operations and Methods

As we mentioned in Module 1, strings are a sequence of characters. The characters in a string can be enclosed in either single (') or double (") quotes. This does not make a difference. A string enclosed in single quotes is completely identical to one enclosed in double quotes is shown in **Snippet 2.24**.

Snippet 2.24

```
>>> "a string"
'a string'
>>> 'foobar'
'foobar'
>>>
```

A double-quoted string can contain single quotes as shown in **Snippet 2.25**.

Snippet 2.25

```
>>> "Susan's"
"Susan's"
>>>
```

A single-quoted string can also contain double quotes as shown in **Snippet 2.26**.

Snippet 2.26

```
>>> '"Help!", he exclaimed.'
'"Help!", he exclaimed.'
>>>
```

You can also build a multiline string by enclosing the characters in triple quotes (''' or """). See **Snippet 2.27**.

Snippet 2.27

```
>>> s = """A multiline
string"""
>>> print(s)
A multiline
string
>>> s2 = '''Also a
multiline string
'''
>>> print(s2)
Also a
multiline string
>>>
```

Also, as you saw in Module 1, you can use the ***** operator to repeat strings as shown in **Snippet 2.28**.

Snippet 2.28

```
>>> print('Alibaba and the', 'thieves ' * 40)
Alibaba and the thieves thieves thieves thieves thieves thieves thieves
thieves thieves thieves thieves thieves thieves thieves thieves thieves
thieves thieves thieves thieves thieves thieves thieves thieves thieves
thieves thieves thieves thieves thieves thieves thieves thieves thieves
thieves thieves thieves thieves thieves thieves
>>>
```

And, you can use the + operator to concatenate strings as shown in **Snippet 2.29**.

Snippet 2.29

```
>>> "I " + "love " + "Python"
'I love Python'
>>>
```

 NOTE Concatenation will join the two strings just as they are, and will not add spaces; thus, we add a space at the end for each string that forms a word in the example shown in Snippet 2.29.

Python strings are *immutable*. This means that once they are assigned to a variable, their value cannot be changed. Consider **Snippet 2.30**.

Snippet 2.30

```
>>> string = "flip flop "
>>> string * 8   # a spider wearing slippers
'flip flop flip flop flip flop flip flop flip flop flip flop flip flop flip
flop '
```

After we print the original value, we will see that the string's original value remains unchanged as shown in **Snippet 2.31**.

Snippet 2.31

```
>>> print(string)
flip flop
```

The same is applicable for all string operations; they do not change any part of the string. See **Snippet 2.32**.

Snippet 2.32

```
>>> hello = "Hello "
>>> world = "World"
>>> hello + world
'Hello World'
>>> hello
'Hello '
```

To *change* the string in Snippet 2.32, we would have to reassign the variable to the new string as shown in **Snippet 2.33**.

Snippet 2.33

```
>>> hello = hello + world
>>> hello
'Hello World'
```

Lesson 2.2.2 Indexing

Python strings can be indexed. Like most languages, the first character in the sequence in the string is at the index 0.

Consider the string `Python is fun`. The table in **Figure 2.6** shows the index of each character in the string. Characters in the string are indexed in two ways—left to right, which starts at 0, and right to left, which starts at −1.

Figure 2.6   String Indices

0	1	2	3	4	5	6	7	8	9	10	11	12
P	y	t	h	o	n		i	s		f	u	n
−13	−12	−11	−10	−9	−8	−7	−6	−5	−4	−3	−2	−1

To get a character from a string, you can use the standard [] syntax shown in **Snippet 2.34**.

Snippet 2.34

```
>>> s = "Python is fun"
>>> s[0]
'P'
>>> print(s[7], s[8])
i s
>>> s[-1]
'n'
>>> s[-13]
'P'
```

If we try to get a character from an index that doesn't exist, Python will raise an IndexError. In **Snippet 2.35**, we are trying to get a character in an index that is larger than the size of the string itself.

Snippet 2.35

```
>>> s = "foobar"
>>> s[100]
Traceback (most recent call last):
  File "<stdin>", line 1, in <module>
IndexError: string index out of range
>>>
```

Lesson 2.2.3 Slicing

Additionally, you can access characters within a range of indices in a string and get a slice/substring of that string. Slicing syntax is in the following format: string[start_index : end_index].

Note that the returned substring doesn't include the character at the end index, but instead, every character up to it, as shown in **Snippet 2.36**.

Snippet 2.36

```
>>> string = "championships"
>>> string[0:5]
'champ'
>>> string[5:9]
'ions'
>>> string[-5:-1]
'ship'
```

Python allows you to omit the start or end index when slicing a string. This is demonstrated in **Snippet 2.37**.

Snippet 2.37

```
>>> string = "foobar"
>>> string[3:]
'bar'
>>> string[:3]
'foo'
```

In Snippet 2.37, we can see that when we pass just the start index while slicing, Python automatically slices the string up to the last index. If we pass only the end index, it slices every character from the start of the string up to that end index.

Test yourself on this concept by completing Lab Activity 2.2A: String Slicing.

Lesson 2.2.4 Length

The length of a string is determined by the number of characters there are inside of it. In Python, you can get the length of a string by using the built-in `len()` function, which takes a string as its parameter and returns an integer. In **Snippet 2.43**, we can see that the length of the string is 44 characters.

Snippet 2.43

```
>>> question = "Who was the first Beatle to leave the group?"
>>> len(question)
44
>>>
```

An empty string would have a length of 0 as shown in **Snippet 2.44**.

Snippet 2.44

```
>>> empty = ""
>>> len(empty)
0
>>>
```

Lesson 2.2.5 String Formatting

String formatting is important when you want to build new strings that are using existing values. Python provides several ways to format text strings. The most popular of these are string interpolation, the `str.format()` method, and % formatting.

STRING INTERPOLATION

In Python 3.6, support for string interpolation was added. String interpolation is the process of evaluating a string that has placeholders. These placeholders can hold expressions that yield a value, which is then placed inside the string. Special kinds of strings, known as **f-strings (formatted strings)**, are used during string interpolation. These strings are prefixed with an `f` to denote how they are meant to be interpreted. An example is shown in **Snippet 2.45**.

Snippet 2.45

```
>>> pie = 3.14
>>> f"I ate some {pie} and it was yummy!"
'I ate some 3.14 and it was yummy!'
>>>
```

NOTE   If you omit the f prefix, the string will be interpreted literally, as it appears.

To insert the variable, we need to place curly braces that contain the expression we want to put inside the string. This can be any valid Python expression. An example is shown in **Snippet 2.46**.

Snippet 2.46

```
>>> number = 7
>>> f"{number+1} is just a number."
'8 is just a number.'
>>>
```

Compared to the other methods that Python offers, Python string interpolation provides powerful, declarative, and more intuitive formatting of your strings. This should be the de facto way to format strings when using Python 3.6+.

THE STR.FORMAT() METHOD

The str.format() method can be found on every string instance. It allows you to insert different values in positions within the string. This method works similarly to interpolation, except for the fact that you can't put expressions into the placeholders, and you have to pass in the values for insertion in the method call. The syntax for this is shown in **Snippet 2.47**.

Snippet 2.47

```
>>> fruit = "bananas"
>>> "I love {}".format(fruit)
'I love bananas'
>>>
```

In the string shown in Snippet 2.47, we put curly braces in the positions where we want to put our values. When we call the format method, it takes that first argument (our variable, fruit), and replaces the curly braces with its value. You can also pass multiple values in.

The values can be any kind of object. An example is shown in **Snippet 2.48**.

Snippet 2.48

```
>>> age = 40
>>> years = 10
>>> string = "In {} years, I'll be {}"
>>> string.format(years, age)
"In 10 years I'll be 40"
>>>
```

If the Python version you are using doesn't support string interpolation, this should be the method that you use.

% FORMATTING

An old, deprecated way of formatting strings, which you might end up seeing in old code, is the C language style % formatting. In this method, you use the % operator to pass in values. Inside the string, you use the % character, followed by a format specifier, to declare how the value should be inserted; for example, %s for string, or %d for integers as shown in **Snippet 2.49**.

Snippet 2.49

```
>>> number = 3
>>> pets = "cats"
>>> "They have %d %s" % (number, pets)
'They have 3 cats'
```

This method is inflexible and is harder to use correctly, and thus, it should generally be avoided.

Lesson 2.2.6 String Methods

Aside from the format method, string instances have a couple of useful methods that can be used to transform and inspect strings. We will demonstrate a few of the common ones. You can read through the Python documentation for more information on string methods.

STR.CAPITALIZE()

The str.capitalize() method returns a copy of the string with the first letter capitalized and the rest in lowercase as shown in **Snippet 2.50**.

Snippet 2.50

```
>>> "HELLO".capitalize()
'Hello'
>>> "hello".capitalize()
'Hello'
```

STR.LOWER()

The str.lower() method returns a copy of the string with all characters converted to lowercase as shown in **Snippet 2.51**.

Snippet 2.51

```
>>> "WORLD".lower()
'world'
>>> "wOrLd".lower()
'world'
```

STR.UPPER()

The `str.upper()` method returns a copy of the string with all characters converted to uppercase as shown in **Snippet 2.52**.

Snippet 2.52

```
>>> "abcd".upper()
'ABCD'
>>> "EfGhi".upper()
'EFGHI'
>>>
```

STR.STARTSWITH()

The `str.startswith()` method checks whether a string starts with the specified prefix. The prefix can contain one or more characters, and is case-sensitive. The method returns a Boolean, `True` or `False`. An example is shown in **Snippet 2.53**.

Snippet 2.53

```
>>> "Python".startswith("Py")
True
>>>
```

STR.ENDSWITH()

The `str.endswith()` method is just like the `startswith` method, but it checks that the string ends with the specified suffix as shown in **Snippet 2.54**.

Snippet 2.54

```
>>> "Python".endswith("on")
True
>>>
```

STR.STRIP()

The `str.strip()` method returns a copy of the string with the leading and trailing characters removed. The method also takes an argument that is a string, specifying the set of characters to be removed. This method is also case-sensitive. If no arguments are passed to it, it removes all of the trailing and leading whitespaces.

This can be useful when sanitizing data. See **Snippet 2.55**.

Snippet 2.55

```
>>> "Championship".strip("ship")
'Champion'
>>> "repair".strip("r")
'epai'
>>> "  John Doe  ".strip()
'John Doe'
>>>
```

STR.REPLACE()

The `str.replace()` method takes two substrings as arguments (old and new), then returns a copy of the string with all of the occurrences of the old substring replaced with the new one. Note that the method is case-sensitive. An example is shown in **Snippet 2.56**.

Snippet 2.56

```
>>> "Cashewnuts".replace("Cashew", "Coco")
'Coconuts'
>>> "Emacs".replace("Emacs", "Vim")
"Vim"
>>>
```

You don't have to remember all of the string methods as you can always refer to the documentation to see what methods strings support. To do this in the interpreter, run the `help` command as shown in **Snippet 2.57**.

Snippet 2.57

```
>>> help(str)
```

You should see the output shown in **Figure 2.7**, which you can browse through.

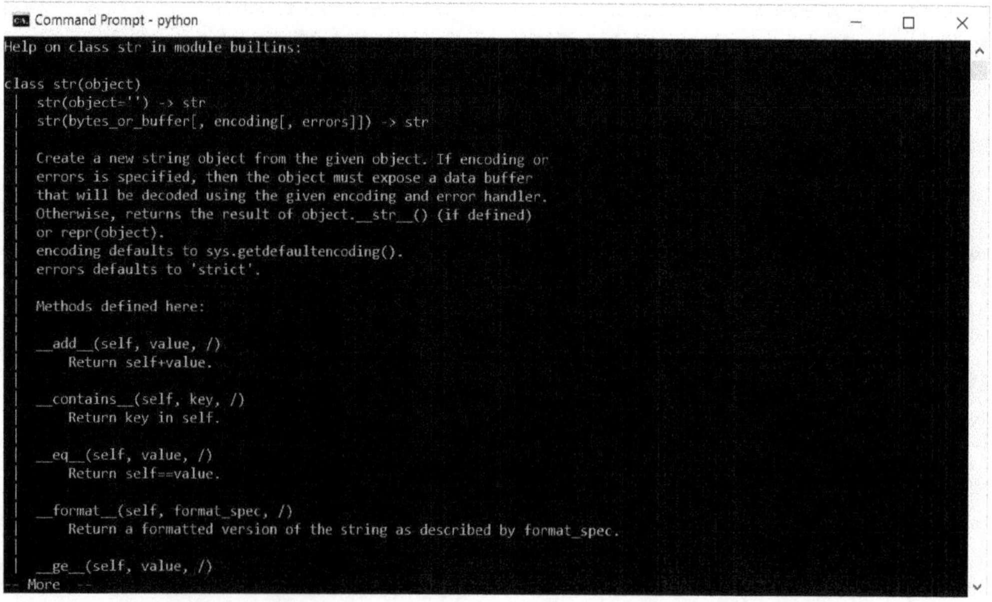

Figure 2.7   Output of help(str)

Test yourself on this concept by completing Lab Activity 2.2B: Working with Strings.

Reviewing what we have learned about strings, we should remember that the characters in a string are indexed, and you can access characters in each index. Python string indices start at 0. You can also access characters within a range of indices by slicing the string. Of the different string formatting methods that Python allows for, you should use string interpolation when using Python versions 3.6+, and the `str.format()` method otherwise.

Lesson 2.2.7 Escape Sequences

An escape sequence is a sequence of characters that does not represent its literal meaning when inside of a string. An escape character tells the interpreter/compiler to interpret the next character(s) in a special way and ignore its usual meaning, thus creating an escape sequence.

In Python, the escape character is the backslash (\). For example, adding \n inside a string will tell the interpreter to interpret a new line inside the string, instead of the literal letter n as shown in **Snippet 2.58**.

Snippet 2.58

```
>>> print("Hello\nWorld")
Hello
World
>>>
```

You can escape quotes inside a string, so that they are not interpreted as closing quotes as shown in **Snippet 2.59**.

Snippet 2.59

```
>>> 'Weekend at Bernie's'
  File "<stdin>", line 1
    'Weekend at Bernie's'
                        ^
SyntaxError: invalid syntax
>>> 'Weekend at Bernie\'s'
"Weekend at Bernie's"
>>>
```

Figure 2.9 shows the full list of valid escape sequences in Python.

Figure 2.9   Escape sequences

Escape Sequence	Definition
\newline	Backlash and newline ignored
\\	Backlash (\)
\'	Single quote (')
\"	Double quote (")
\a	ASCII Bell (BEL)
\b	ASCII Backspace (BS)
\f	ASCII Formfeed (FF)
\n	ASCII Linefeed (LF)
\r	ASCII Carriage Return (CR)
\t	ASCII Horizontal Tab (TAB)
\v	ASCII Vertical Tab (VT)
\ooo	Character with octal value ooo
\xhh	Character with hex value hh

Practice this concept by completing Practice Exercise 2.2: Using Escape Sequences.

Escape sequences in **strings** tell the program to perform a function or command, such as insert a new line, ignore quotes occurring in strings, prompt the terminal to emit an audible signal, and several other functions.

Let's review what we have learned about strings:

- Strings are a sequence of characters.
- Strings can be enclosed in either single quotes (') or double quotes (").
- Multiline strings can be enclosed in either triple single quotes (''') or triple double quotes (""").
- Strings are immutable.
- Characters in a string are indexed, and you can access each character by index.
- The first element in a string is at the index 0.
- Substrings in a string can be accessed by slicing.
- Formatting strings allows you to insert values into a string.
- Strings come with **several** handy built-in methods for transforming or inspecting the string.
- Escape sequences in strings tell the program to perform a function or command.

> Test yourself on this concept by completing Lab Activity 2.2C: Manipulating Strings.

LESSON 2.3 LISTS

This is part one of two lessons in this course that focus on lists. This part will act as an introduction, and will not cover the various methods that list objects have, such as `extend()`, `remove()`, `pop()`, and several others. We will go through the second section on lists in a later module.

Lesson 2.3.1 List Operations

In Python, arrays (or the closest abstraction of them) are known as **lists**. Lists are an aggregate data type, meaning that they are composed of other data types. Lists are similar to strings, in that the values inside them are indexed, and they have a length property and a count of the objects inside of them. In Python, lists are heterogeneous, in that they can hold values of different types. In contrast to how arrays are in most languages, Python lists are also mutable, meaning that you can change the values inside of them, adding and removing items on the go.

Lists can be likened to a wardrobe. Wardrobes can hold multiple items of clothing, clothes of different kinds, and even shoes. Wardrobes provide a convenient storage space for the easy retrieval of your clothes, so that you don't have to look for them all around the house. If we didn't have a list, we would have to keep track of dozens of separate variables. Like wardrobes, lists provide a convenient collection of related objects.

Lists are made with its comma-separated elements enclosed in square brackets; for example, see **Snippet 2.61**.

Snippet 2.61

```
>>> digits = [1, 2, 3, 4, 5, 6, 7, 8, 9, 0]
>>> digits
[1, 2, 3, 4, 5, 6, 7, 8, 9, 0]
>>> letters = ["a", "b", "c", "d"]
>>> letters
['a', 'b', 'c', 'd']
>>> mixed_list = [1, 3.14159, "Spring", "Summer", [1, 2, 3, 4]]
>>> mixed_list
[1, 3.14159, 'Spring', 'Summer', [1, 2, 3, 4]]
>>>
```

As you can see in Snippet 2.61, lists can also contain other lists within them. You can also get the number of elements in a list by using the `len()` function as shown in **Snippet 2.62**.

Snippet 2.62

```
>>> len(["a", "b", "c", "d"])
4
>>>
```

INDEXING

Like strings, lists can also be indexed. The first element in a list starts at the index 0 as shown in **Snippet 2.63**.

Snippet 2.63

```
>>> fruits = ["apples", "bananas", "strawberries", "mangoes", "pears"]
>>> fruits[3]
'mangoes'
```

Negative indices can be used as well, as shown in **Snippet 2.64**.

Snippet 2.64

```
>>> fruits[-1]
'pears'
>>>
```

SLICING

Lists can also be sliced. The slicing operation always returns a new list that has been derived from the old list. The syntax remains as `list[start_index : end_index ]`. As with string slicing, the element at the end index isn't included in the result as shown in **Snippet 2.65**.

Snippet 2.65

```
>>> my_list = [10, 20, 30, 40, 50, 60, 70]
>>> my_list[4:5]
[50]
>>> my_list[5:]
[60, 70]
>>>
```

Omitting the end index and providing only the start index will slice everything from the start to the end of the list, while omitting the start index and giving only the end index will slice everything from the start index to the end index as shown in **Snippet 2.66**.

Snippet 2.66

```
>>> my_list = [10, 20, 30, 40, 50, 60, 70]
>>> my_list[5:]
[60, 70]
>>> my_list[:4]
[10, 20, 30, 40]
>>>
```

CONCATENATION

Additionally, you can add two lists together by using the + operator. The elements of all of the lists being concatenated are brought together inside one list as shown in **Snippet 2.67**.

Snippet 2.67

```
>>> [1, 2, 3] + [4, 5, 6]
[1, 2, 3, 4, 5, 6]
>>> ["a", "b", "c"] + [1, 2.0, 3]
['a', 'b', 'c', 1, 2.0, 3]
>>>
```

CHANGING VALUES IN A LIST

Because lists are mutable, you can change the value in a list by assigning whatever is at that index as shown in **Snippet 2.68**.

Snippet 2.68

```
>>> names = ["Eva", "Keziah", "John", "Diana"]
>>> names[2] = "Jean"
>>> names
['Eva', 'Keziah', 'Jean', 'Diana']
>>>
```

Note that it is possible to add any type of value to a list, regardless of what types of values it contains. For example, you can add an integer to a list of strings or a string to a list of integers, and so on.

You can also use the `list.append()` method to insert a value at the end of a list as shown in **Snippet 2.69**.

Snippet 2.69

```
>>> planets = ["Mercury", "Venus", "Earth", "Mars", "Jupiter", "Saturn",
"Uranus", "Neptune"]
>>> planets.append("Planet X")
>>> planets
['Mercury', 'Venus', 'Earth', 'Mars', 'Jupiter', 'Saturn', 'Uranus',
'Neptune', 'Planet X']
```

Finally, you can assign slices of a list. This replaces the target slice with whatever you assign, regardless of the initial size of the list:

Snippet 2.70

```
>>> alphanumeric_list = [1, 2, 3, 4, 5, 6, 7, 8, 9, 0]
>>> alphanumeric_list[4:7]
[5, 6, 7]
>>> alphanumeric_list[4:7] = ["a", "b", "c"]
>>> alphanumeric_list
[1, 2, 3, 4, 'a', 'b', 'c', 8, 9, 0]
```

An important thing to note is that when you assign a variable to a list, the variable points it to an object in memory. If you assign another variable to the variable that references that list, the new variable also references that same list object in memory. Any changes made using either reference will always change the same list object in memory.

> Practice this concept by completing Practice Exercise 2.3: List References.

Both lists will change because both variables reference the same object.

We have seen that lists are collections of values. Python lists are mutable. There are multiple operations that you can carry out on lists, such as accessing elements by index, slicing elements, getting the count of elements inside a list, concatenation, and changing values, either by index, appending, or replacing slices of the list.

> Test yourself on this concept by completing Lab Activity 2.3: Working with Lists.

LESSON 2.4 BOOLEANS

Boolean data types are values that can only be one of two values, True or False. For example, the proposition *100 is more than 5* is *True*, and thus, it would have a True Boolean value. On the other hand, the proposition *The sky is green* is *False*, and thus, it would have a False Boolean value.

Booleans are largely associated with control statements, as they change the flow of the program, depending on the truthfulness of the specified quantities.

In Python, True and False are used to represent the two Boolean constants as shown in **Snippet 2.75**.

Snippet 2.75

```
>>> True
True
>>> False
False
>>> print(type(True), type(False))
<class 'bool'> <class 'bool'>
```

We can see that the type of each expression is bool (short for Boolean). Like all other types, Booleans have operators that you can apply.

Lesson 2.4.1 Comparison Operators

Comparison operators compare the values of objects or the objects' identities themselves. The objects don't need to be of the same type. There are eight comparison operators in Python. They are shown in **Figure 2.13**.

Figure 2.13   Comparison operators

Operator	Meaning
<	Less than
<=	Less than or equal to
>	Greater than
>=	Greater than or equal to
==	Equal to
!=	Not equal to
is	Object identity
is not	Negated object identity

Snippet 2.76 includes some example uses of these operators.

Snippet 2.76

```
>>> 10 < 1
False
>>> len("open") <= 4
True
>>> 10 > 1
True
>>> len(["banana"]) >= 0
True
>>> "Foobar" == "Foobar"
True
>>> "Foobar" != "Foobar"
False
>>>
```

Now, consider the code in **Snippet 2.77**.

Snippet 2.77

```
>>> l = [1, 2, 3]
>>> l2 = l
>>> l is l2
True
>>> l is not None
True
>>>
```

First, we create a list, l, and then assign the variable l2 to that same list. This creates a reference for the list. Thus, the statement l is l2 is True, because both variables reference the same object in the memory.

The statement l is not None evaluates to True, as well, because l points to something in the memory, and therefore, it isn't null. None is the Python equivalent of null.

Lesson 2.4.2 Logical Operators

We use logic in **everyday** life. Consider the following statements:

- *I'll have juice OR water if there isn't any juice.*
- *The knife has to be sharpened AND polished for the chef to use it.*
- *I am NOT tired; therefore, I will stay awake.*

Each of these statements has a condition. The condition for having water is if there isn't any juice available. The chef will only use the knife if two conditions are met, that is, that it is sharpened and that it is polished. The condition for staying awake is only if the condition of being tired has not been met.

In the same way, we have logical operators that combine Boolean expressions in Python: not, and, and or, as described in the table shown in **Figure 2.14**.

Figure 2.14   Logical operators

Operator	Result
not x	Returns false if x is true, else false
x and y	Returns x if x is false, else returns y
x or y	Returns y if x is false, else returns x

and is a short-circuit operator, in that it only evaluates the second argument if the first one is True. or is also a short-circuit operator, in that it will only evaluate the second argument if the first one is False.

Snippet 2.78 shows an example of and.

Snippet 2.78

```
>>> fruits = ["banana", "mangoes", "apples"]
>>> wants_fruits = True
>>> len(fruits) > 0 and wants_fruits
True
>>>
```

The code shown in **Snippet 2.79** shows or in action.

Snippet 2.79

```
>>> value_1 = 5
>>> value_2 = 0
>>> value_1 > 0 or value_2 > 0
True
>>>
```

Finally, **Snippet 2.80** shows an example of not.

Snippet 2.80

```
>>> not True
False
>>> not False
True
>>>
```

Lesson 2.4.3 Membership Operators

The operators in and not in test for membership. All sequences (for example, lists and strings) support this operator. For lists, these operators go through each element to see whether the element being searched for is within the list. For strings, the operators check whether the substring can be found within the string. The return values for these operators are True or False.

Snippet 2.81 shows how they work.

Snippet 2.81

```
>>> numbers = [1, 2, 3, 4, 5]
>>> 3 in numbers
True
>>> 100 in numbers
False
>>> sentence = "I like beef, mutton and pork"
>>> "chicken" not in sentence
True
>>> "beef" not in sentence
False
>>>
```

Boolean data types are values that can be either True or False. You can compare the values of two objects by using comparison operators, and you can combine or alter Boolean expressions by using logical operators. Membership operators are used to assert whether an element can be found in a sequence or container type object.

Test yourself on this concept by completing Lab Activity 2.4: Using Boolean Operators.

SUMMARY

In this module, we took an in-depth look at the basic data types that Python supports. We started with numerical data types and their related operators. We then covered strings and looked at string indexing, slicing, and formatting. Then, we moved on and took a brief look at lists (also known as arrays) and Booleans, as well as Boolean operators.

In Module 3, we will begin our journey into learning how to control the flow of our programs by using control statements and loops.

CONTROL STATEMENTS

MODULE OBJECTIVES

BY THE END OF THIS MODULE, YOU WILL BE ABLE TO:

1. Describe the different control statements in Python
2. Control program execution flow using control statements such as `if` and `while`
3. Use looping structures in your Python programs
4. Implement branching within looping structures such as `for` and `range`
5. Implement breaking out of loops

INTRODUCTION

This module describes the Python program flow and how we can change the flow of execution using control statements such as if, while, for, and range.

Previously in this course, we covered the following topics:

- The Python interpreter
- Python syntax
- Values and data types

In this module, we are going to build on the knowledge that we have acquired to dive deeper into the beautiful language that is Python. In this module, we will explore how Python handles control statements—in simple terms, how Python handles decision making, for instance, resulting in *True* if 2 + 3 = 5.

In this module, we will also dive deeper into program flow control. In particular, we will look at how we can run code repeatedly or in a loop.

Specifically, we will cover the following topics:

- Python program flow
- Python control statements, that is, `if` and `while`
- The differences between `if` and `while`

- The `for` loop
- The `range` function
- Nesting loops
- Breaking out of loops

LESSON 3.1 CONTROL STATEMENTS

Like most programming languages, Python supports a number of ways to control the execution of a program by using control statements. Some of them might already be familiar, while others are unique to Python either in terms of syntax or execution.

We will delve into controlling program flow and start working on building more structured programs. This should also prepare us for learning various kinds of loops later in this module. To start us off, we are going to define some terms:

- Program flow
- Control statement

Lesson 3.1.1 Program Flow

Program flow describes the way in which statements in code are executed. This also includes the priority given to different elements.

Python uses a simple top-down program flow. This means that code is executed in sequence from the top of the file to the bottom. Each line has to wait until all of the lines that come before it have completed execution before its own execution can begin.

This top-down program flow makes it easy to understand and debug Python programs, as you can visually step through the code and see where things are failing.

In a top-down scenario, a problem is broken down into simple modules, each responsible for a part of the solution and closely related to one another. For instance, consider a salary calculation. There could be a module responsible for each of the following:

- Tax computation
- Debt computation (if needed)
- Net amount computation

Lesson 3.1.2 Control Statement

Having defined the program flow, we can now understand what a control statement is.

A control statement is a structure in code that conditionally changes the program flow. A control statement achieves this change by conditionally executing different parts of code. A control statement can also be used to repeatedly and conditionally execute some code.

You can think of a control statement as a traffic officer at a junction who only lets traffic through if the exit is clear. In this case, checking whether the exit is clear would be the condition.

The two main control statements in Python are:

- `if`
- `while`

LESSON 3.2 THE IF STATEMENT

An `if` statement allows you to execute a block of code if a condition is true. Otherwise, it can run an alternative block of code in its `else` clause.

The `else` clause of an `if` statement is optional.

You can chain multiple `if` statements that check for multiple conditions one after the other and execute a different block of code when the various conditions are true. When doing this you could use the `elif` statement. `elif` is a combination of `else` and `if`, and enables a broader comparison scope through chaining multiple `if` statements.

The basic syntax of an `if` statement is shown in **Snippet 3.1**.

Snippet 3.1

```
if condition:
    # Run this code if the condition evaluates to True
else:
    # Run this code if the condition evaluates to False
```

As you can see, the `if` statement allows you to branch the execution of code based on a condition. If the condition evaluates to true, we execute the code in the `if` block. If the condition evaluates to false, we execute the code in the `else` block.

> Practice this concept by completing Practice Exercise 3.2: Using the if Statement.

An `if` statement is used when you want to conditionally execute different blocks of code. The `if` statement is especially useful when there are multiple different blocks of code that could be executed, depending on multiple conditions.

> Test yourself on this concept by completing Lab Activity 3.2: Working with the if Statement.

LESSON 3.3 THE WHILE STATEMENT

A `while` statement allows you to execute a block of code repeatedly, as long as a condition remains true. That is to say, *as long as condition X remains true, execute this code.*

A `while` statement can also have an `else` clause that will be executed exactly once when the condition, *X*, is no longer true. This can be read as follows: *As long as X remains true, execute this block of code, else, execute this other block of code immediately when that condition is no longer true.*

For instance, consider the traffic officer we mentioned earlier, who could be letting traffic through while the exit is clear, and as soon as it is not clear, he stops the drivers from exiting.

Snippet 3.13 shows the basic syntax of a `while` statement.

Snippet 3.13

```
while condition:
    # Run this code while condition is true
    # Replace the "condition" above with an actual condition
    # This code keeps running as long as the condition evaluates to True
else:
    # Run the code in here once the condition is no longer true
    # This code only runs one time unlike the code in the while block
```

As mentioned, this can be read as: *As long as the condition is true, execute the first block of code, and if the condition is not true, execute the second block of code.*

Practice this concept by completing Practice Exercise 3.3A: Using the while Statement.

Practice this concept by completing Practice Exercise 3.3B: Using while to Keep a Program Running.

The `while` loop is used in the following cases:

- When we must wait for a condition to be satisfied before continuing execution
- When a user's input is required—as seen in Practice Exercise 3.3B.

Test yourself on this concept by completing Lab Activity 3.3: Working with the while Statement.

LESSON 3.4 WHILE VERSUS IF

The main difference between an `if` and a `while` statement is that an `if` statement gives you the opportunity to branch the execution of code once based on a condition. The code in the `if` block is only executed once. For instance, if a value is greater than another, an `if` statement will branch out and execute a computation, and then proceed with the program's flow or exit.

A `while` statement, however, gives you the opportunity to run a block of code multiple times as long as a condition evaluates to true. This means that a `while` statement will, for example, execute a computation as long as value A is greater than value B and only proceed with the program flow when A is no longer greater than B.

In this sense, a `while` statement can be considered a loop. We will look at looping structures next.

LESSON 3.5 LOOPS

In Python, loops (just as in any other language) are a way to execute a specific block of code several times. In particular, loops are used to iterate or loop over what we call iterables.

For the purposes of this module, we can define an iterable as follows:

- Anything that can be looped over (that is, you can loop over a string or a file)
- Anything that can appear on the right-hand side of a `for` loop, for example, `for x in iterable`

A few examples of common iterables include the following:

- Strings
- Lists
- Dictionaries
- Files

You can think of an iterable as a collection of homogeneous things that have been grouped together to form a large collective. The individuals in the group have the same properties, and when they are combined, they form something new.

Consider the example of cars in a car lot. We can consider the car lot as the collection or iterable and the individual cars as the constituent members of the car lot. If you were shopping for a car, you would probably have a couple of qualities that you are looking for. You walk into the car lot and start going from car to car looking for one that satisfies your conditions or comes as close as possible to satisfying your conditions. The act of going from car to car and repeating the aforementioned inspection operation is basically what looping is.

Loops allow us to deconstruct iterables and perform operations on their constituent members or even convert them into new data structures. The possibilities are endless when you start using loops.

LESSON 3.6 THE FOR LOOP

The `for` loop in Python is also referred to as the `for...in` loop. This is because of its unique syntax that differs a bit from `for` loops in other languages.

A `for` loop is used when you have a block of code that you would like to execute repeatedly a given number of times. For example, multiplying an iterable value, or dividing the value by another if the iterable value is still present in the loop.

The loop differs from a `while` statement in that in a `for` loop, the repeated code block runs a predetermined number of times, while with a `while` statement, the code runs an arbitrary number of times as long as a condition is satisfied.

The basic syntax of a `for` loop is shown in **Snippet 3.33**.

Snippet 3.33

```
# Iterable can be anything that can be looped over e.g. a list
# Member is a single constituent of the iterable e.g. an entry in a list
for member in iterable:
    # Execute this code for each constituent member of the iterable
    pass
```

As shown in Snippet 3.33, the `for` loop allows you to go through all constituent members of an iterable and run a block of code for each. This code could be anything from a simple summation of the values to more complex manipulations and analysis. Again, the possibilities are endless, and having the ability to easily access iterables like this will prove invaluable as you start building more complex programs in Python.

Practice this concept by completing Practice Exercise 3.6: Using the for Loop.

Lesson 3.6.1 Using else

As with a `while` statement, an `else` statement can also be optionally used with a `for` loop. In this case, the code inside the `else` block will be executed exactly once when the loop exits cleanly. Exiting cleanly means that the loop went through all the members of the iterable without breaking.

Snippet 3.40 shows the script we created in Practice Exercise 3.6 with an `else` clause added.

Snippet 3.40

```
# Create a list with number 1 through 10
numbers = [1, 2, 3, 4, 5, 6, 7, 8, 9, 10]

# Loop through the list of numbers
for num in numbers:
    # Calculate the square of the number
    square = num * num
    # Print out a string showing the number and its calculated square
    print(num ,'squared is', square)
else:
    print('The last number was', num)
```

The `else` clause is added to the very bottom of the loop. The output from Snippet 3.40 is shown in **Snippet 3.41**.

Snippet 3.41

```
1 squared is 1
2 squared is 4
3 squared is 9
4 squared is 16
5 squared is 25
6 squared is 36
7 squared is 49
8 squared is 64
9 squared is 81
10 squared is 100
The last number was 10
```

As we can see, the `else` clause is executed only once and only after the rest of the code has run successfully. It is also important to note that although it may not seem like it, the `else` clause has access to all the variables created within the `for` loop. This can prove very valuable for debugging and handling error conditions in our code.

LESSON 3.7 THE RANGE FUNCTION

Python's `range` function is a built-in function that generates a list of numbers. This list is mostly used to iterate over using a `for` loop.

This function is used when you want to perform an action a predetermined number of times, where you may or may not care about the index. For instance, you could use a range to find all even numbers between 0 and 100, where Python will list or print out all even numbers in that range, excluding 100, even though it is an even number. You can also use it to iterate over a list (or another iterable) while keeping track of the index.

The basic syntax of the range function is shown in **Snippet 3.42**.

Snippet 3.42

```
range([start], stop, [step])
```

Here is a breakdown of what each parameter does:

- start: This is the starting number of the sequence.
- stop: This means generate numbers up to but not including this number.
- step: This is the difference between each number in the sequence.

As a general rule, when a parameter is enclosed in square brackets [] in the function definition, it means that that particular parameter is optional when you are calling the function.

This means that the only required parameter when calling the range function is the stop parameter, and the default call to the function can have just that one parameter.

Now, let's look at some calls to the range function and their corresponding output. First, perform a call with just the stop parameter included as shown in **Snippet 3.43**.

Snippet 3.43

```
range(10)
```

The range(10) call basically tells the function to generate numbers from 0 to 10, but not including 10. To view the numbers, we would have to cast the range object into a list object. The output of this call is shown in **Snippet 3.44**.

Snippet 3.44

```
>>> range(10)
range(0, 10)
>>> list(range(10))
[0, 1, 2, 3, 4, 5, 6, 7, 8, 9]
```

Please note that the range function starts at zero if a start parameter is not provided.

What if we wanted to create a list from 1 to 10? To achieve this, you would have to include the start parameter of the range function. You would also have to change the stop parameter, too. Remember that the stop parameter is not included in the final generated list.

The pseudo-code for what you want to achieve is: *Generate a list of all numbers from 1 to 10.*

Snippet 3.45 shows how we do it.

Snippet 3.45

```
>>> list(range(1, 11))
[1, 2, 3, 4, 5, 6, 7, 8, 9, 10]
```

How is the step parameter used? The step parameter defines the difference between each number in the generated list. If you set step to 5, the difference between each number on the list will be a constant of 5. This can be useful when you want to generate a very particular set of numbers between any given two points.

Let's write a piece of code that generates a list of all even numbers between 2 and 20 inclusive. Here, we can see the application of the `step` parameter. We will use it to make sure that the difference between each number is 2, thus ensuring that the final list will only contain even numbers.

Snippet 3.46 shows how we can do it.

Snippet 3.46

```
>>> list(range(2, 21, 2))
>>> [2, 4, 6, 8, 10, 12, 14, 16, 18, 20]
```

Conversely, you can generate a list of all odd numbers between 1 and 20 by tweaking the code a bit and changing that first parameter 2 to 1 so that the function starts at 1 instead of 2 as shown in **Snippet 3.47**.

Snippet 3.47

```
>>> list(range(1, 21, 2))
>>> [1, 3, 5, 7, 9, 11, 13, 15, 17, 19]
```

Now that we are familiar with how `range` works, we can look at some practical applications of `range` in a real program. Consider the code shown in **Snippet 3.48**.

Snippet 3.48

```
for num in range(1, 11):
    print(num ,'squared is', num * num)
```

This is a rewrite of the code that we used in Practice Exercise 3.6 with the `for` loop. The `for` loop code is shown in **Snippet 3.49** for comparison.

Snippet 3.49

```
numbers = [1, 2, 3, 4, 5, 6, 7, 8, 9, 10]

for num in numbers:
    square = num * num
    print(num ,'squared is', square)
```

It is evident that we are able to achieve the same result using far less code and without having to initialize variables that may not be used outside of this loop. This helps keep our code clean.

Test yourself on this concept by completing Lab Activity 3.7: The for Loop and the range Function.

LESSON 3.8 NESTING LOOPS

Nesting can be defined as the practice of placing loops inside other loops. Although it is frowned upon in some applications, sometimes it is necessary to nest loops to achieve the desired effect.

Nested loops are important for when you need to access data inside a complex data structure. They can also be used in the comparison of two data structures. For instance, a computation that requires values in two lists would have you loop through both lists and execute the result. It is sometimes necessary to use one or more loops inside another loop to get to that level of granularity.

> Practice this concept by completing Practice Exercise 3.8: Using Nested Loops.

There is no limit to how far you can nest loops, though you should keep code readability in mind when writing nested loops. You don't want to nest so much that you cannot easily deduce what the code does or the expected results of running the code at a glance. Remember, you are writing your code not just for the computer but for future developers who might need to work on it. Oftentimes, this future developer is you in a couple of months. Six months from now you don't want to look at some code that you wrote and not be able to comprehend it. Do yourself a favor: keep it simple.

> Test yourself on this concept by completing Lab Activity 3.8: Nested Loops.

LESSON 3.9 BREAKING OUT OF LOOPS

When running loops, we might want, because of an external factor, to interrupt or intervene in the execution of a loop before it runs its full course. For instance, when writing a function looping though a list of numbers, you may want to break when a defined condition external to the program flow is met. We will demonstrate this further.

Python provides us with three statements that can be used to achieve this:

- `break`
- `continue`
- `pass`

Lesson 3.9.1 The break Statement

The `break` statement allows you to exit a loop based on an external trigger. This means that you can exit the loop based on a condition external to the loop. This statement is usually used in conjunction with a conditional `if` statement.

Snippet 3.59 is an example program that shows the break statement in action.

Snippet 3.59

```
# Loop over all numbers from 1 to 10
for number in range(1,11):
    # If the number is 4, exit the loop
    if number == 4:
        break

    # Calculate the product of number and 2
    product = number * 2
    # Print out the product in a friendly way
    print(number, '* 2 = ', product)

print('Loop completed')
```

The output for the program in Snippet 3.59 is shown in **Snippet 3.60**.

Snippet 3.60

```
1 * 2 =  2
2 * 2 =  4
3 * 2 =  6
Loop completed
```

As shown by the output in Snippet 3.60, the loop exits when number is equal to 4 because of the conditional if number == 4 statement.

Lesson 3.9.2 The continue Statement

The continue statement allows you to skip over the part of a loop where an external condition is triggered, but then goes on to complete the rest of the loop. This means that the current run of the loop will be interrupted, but the program will return to the top of the loop and continue execution from there.

As with the break statement, the continue statement is usually used in conjunction with a conditional if statement.

Snippet 3.61 shows the same code from Snippet 3.59 with the break statement replaced with a continue statement.

Snippet 3.61

```
# Loop over all numbers from 1 to 10
for number in range(1,11):
    # If the number is 4, continue the loop from the top
    if number == 4:
        continue

    # Calculate the product of number and 2
    product = number * 2
    # Print out the product in a friendly way
    print(number, '* 2 = ', product)

print('Loop completed')
```

The output is shown in **Snippet 3.62**.

Snippet 3.62

```
1 * 2 = 2
2 * 2 = 4
3 * 2 = 6
5 * 2 = 10
6 * 2 = 12
7 * 2 = 14
8 * 2 = 16
9 * 2 = 18
10 * 2 = 20
Loop completed
```

Note the difference between the output shown in Snippet 3.62 and the output of the break statement shown in Snippet 3.60. This loop, instead of exiting when it reached 4, simply skips over the rest of the loop when number is 4 and resumes execution at the top of the loop. The product of 4 is, therefore, never printed to the screen, but the rest of the output is printed normally.

Lesson 3.9.3 The pass Statement

The pass statement allows you to handle an external trigger condition without affecting the execution of the loop; the loop will continue to execute as normal unless it hits a break or continue statement somewhere later in the code.

As with the other statements, the pass statement is usually used in conjunction with a conditional if statement.

Snippet 3.63 shows the code from the break statement example, with break replaced with pass.

Snippet 3.63

```
# Loop over all numbers from 1 to 10
for number in range(1,11):
    # If the number is 4, proceed as normal
    if number == 4:
        pass

    # Calculate the product of number and 2
    product = number * 2
    # Print out the product in a friendly way
    print(number, '* 2 = ', product)

print('Loop completed')
```

The output of **Snippet 3.63** is shown in **Snippet 3.64**.

Snippet 3.64

```
1 * 2 = 2
2 * 2 = 4
3 * 2 = 6
4 * 2 = 8
5 * 2 = 10
6 * 2 = 12
7 * 2 = 14
8 * 2 = 16
9 * 2 = 18
10 * 2 = 20
Loop completed
```

As evident, the code encounters the condition but does nothing based on it. The `pass` statement simply tells the program to proceed as normal. The `pass` statement is also mostly used as a placeholder.

Test yourself on this concept by completing Lab Activity 3.9: Breaking Out of Loops.

SUMMARY

In this module, we have learned about how programs in Python flow. We also learned how to control and branch the flow of a Python program by using the two main control statements, that is, `if` and `while`. We have also looked at some practical applications of the two control statements and have seen how they differ in implementation and syntax.

In this module, we have also increased our knowledge of looping structures. We have seen the structure of a `for` loop and looked at practical examples. We have also looked into the `range` function and how it is useful when you need to quickly iterate over a list.

We have also covered how and when to nest loops and how to break out of loops prematurely under different conditions and with differing results by using the `break`, `continue`, and `pass` statements.

Armed with this knowledge, you can now start incorporating more complex structures into your programs.

In the next module, we will look at functions and how to define them, the various types of functions, and how they can help us compartmentalize our code.

FUNCTIONS

MODULE OBJECTIVES

BY THE END OF THIS MODULE, YOU WILL BE ABLE TO:

1. Describe the various function types in Python
2. Define global and local variables
3. Define a function that takes in a variable number of arguments

INTRODUCTION

This module introduces functions in Python. We look at the various types of functions and define our own.

In Module 3 : Control Statements, we covered the following topics:

- How to use looping structures
- How to branch within looping structures
- How to break out of loops

We will continue to build on this knowledge by implementing what we have learned, to build functions in Python.

Functions are an integral part of the Python programming language, and a lot of languages, really. Throughout this book, you have already encountered some built-in functions, especially when dealing with certain data structures.

Functions are an easy way to group a few lines of code that implement a functionality together. This is especially useful if the code in question will be used several times in different parts of your program. You may want to use functions to hide or move some complex code from the main program in a process called abstracting away. You can think of functions as mini-programs within your bigger program that implement specific tasks.

It is important to remember that while it is tempting to tuck a lot of functionality into a single function, it is better to write functions that only perform one specific task. This makes it easier to modularize your code, and, in the long run, it is more maintainable and easier to debug.

Functions may take optional inputs to work with and may optionally return a value or values.

The three main types of functions in Python are as follows:

- Built-in functions
- User-defined functions
- Anonymous functions

LESSON 4.1 BUILT-IN FUNCTIONS

The Python interpreter has a number of functions and types that are always available. These are called **built-in functions**, and they can be used anywhere in your code, without the need of any importation.

Some of the built-in functions that we have already encountered in this course are as follows:

- input([prompt]): This optionally prints the prompt to the terminal. It then reads a line from the input and returns that line.
- print(): Prints objects to the text stream file or the terminal.int(): Returns an integer number converted from a specified value.

For example, we recently used the built-in print() function to output results; **Snippet 4.1** is another simple demonstration.

Snippet 4.1

```
print("Hello world")
```

This results in the output shown in **Snippet 4.2**.

Snippet 4.2

```
Hello world
```

LESSON 4.2 USER-DEFINED FUNCTIONS

As the name suggests, these are functions that are written by the user, to aid them in achieving a specific goal. The main use of functions is to help us organize our programs into logical fragments that work together to solve a specific part of our problem.

The syntax of a Python function is shown in **Snippet 4.3**.

Snippet 4.3

```
def function_name( parameter_one, parameter_two, parameter_n ):
    # Logic goes here
    return
```

To define a function, we can use the following steps:

1. Use the `def` keyword, followed by the function name.
2. Add parameters (if any) to the function within the parentheses. End the function definition with a full colon.
3. Write the logic of the function.
4. Finally, use the `return` keyword to return the output of the function. This is optional, and if it is not included, the function automatically returns `None`.

A user-defined function must have a name. You can give it any name that you like, and it is a good practice to make the name as descriptive of the task that the function achieves as possible. For example, if you are writing a function that calculates the monthly average rainfall from a list of values, it is better to name the function `calculate_monthly_average_rainfall()` than `calculate()`. *Remember, code is written to be read by humans, not computers.* Make it easy for other humans to immediately understand what a function does, just by looking at the name. See the example in **Snippet 4.4**.

Snippet 4.4

```
def calculate_monthly_average_rainfall(list_of_annual_values):
    # Loop over list and calculate average here
    return average
```

Parameters are the information that needs to be passed to the function in order for it to do its work. Parameters are optional, and they are separated by commas and placed between parentheses after the function name. A function can have any number of parameters; there is no limit.

Lesson 4.2.1 Calling a Function

Calling a function means executing the logic that is defined inside of the function. This can be done from the Python interactive prompt, or from within some other part of your code. Functions are often called from other functions.

If we were to call the function that we defined earlier (the one that calculates the monthly rainfall average), it might look like **Snippet 4.5**.

Snippet 4.5

```
annual_values = []
calculate_monthly_average_rainfall(annual_values)
```

Note that the names of the arguments that we pass when we are calling the function in this instance do not have to match the parameter names that the function expects. What is important is that no matter what you pass to the function when calling it, the function will refer to this parameter as `list_of_annual_values` internally.

This transitions us smoothly to our next lesson: global and local variables.

Lesson 4.2.2 Global and Local Variables

Variables that are defined inside of a function body are called **local variables**, as they are only accessible inside the function. They are said to have a local scope.

Variables that are defined outside of a function body are called **global variables**, as they are accessible both outside and inside of the functions. They are said to have a global scope because of this.

Practice this concept by completing Practice Exercise 4.2: Defining Global and Local Variables.

Lesson 4.2.3 Function Return

The `return` statement in Python is used within functions, to actually return something to the caller of the function. Without a `return` statement, every function will return `None`.

Consider the function shown in **Snippet 4.17**.

Snippet 4.17

```
def summation(first, second):
    total = first + second
    print("The total is " + str(total))

summation(10, 20)
```

The output of this code is shown in **Snippet 4.18**.

Snippet 4.18

```
The total is 30
```

Note that the `summation` function, in this case, does not have a `return` statement. As mentioned previously, a `return` statement is not necessary for all functions. The purpose of this function in particular is to print out the total, and in this case, it is not necessary to return anything, as the printing can be done within the function.

However, a `return` statement is required if you need to use the result of calling a function for any further processing in your code. Consider the variation shown in **Snippet 4.19**.

Snippet 4.19

```
def summation(first, second):
    total = first + second
    return total

outer_total = summation(10, 20) * 2

print("Double the total is " + str(outer_total))
```

In this variation, we can see that the `summation` function returns the sum of the passed-in values. This returned value is then multiplied by two and assigned to the `outer_total` variable. This way, the function has, in essence, abstracted away the operation of summing the two numbers.

Of course, this is just a rudimentary example, and with this knowledge, you can begin to build more complex functions and programs.

Lesson 4.2.4 Using main()

Most other programming languages (for example, Java and C++) require a special function, called main(), which tells the operating system what code to execute when a program is invoked. This is not necessary in Python, but you will find that it is a good and logical way to structure a program.

Before the Python interpreter executes our program, it defines a few special variables. One of them is __name__, and it will automatically be set to __main__ if our program will be executed by itself, in a standalone fashion.

However, if our program will be imported by another program, then __name__ will be set to the name of that other program. We can easily determine whether the program is standalone or is being used by another program as an import. Based on that, we can decide to either execute or exclude some of the code in a program.

Snippet 4.20 is an example that uses the main() function.

Snippet 4.20

```python
def summation(first, second):
    total = first + second
    return total

def main():
    outer_total = summation(10, 20) * 2
    print("Double the total is " + str(outer_total))

if __name__ == "__main__":
    main()
```

Without the if __name_ == __main__ check and declaration, our script would still be executable. All we would have to do is declare or call our summation() function.

In Python, there is nothing special about the name main. We could have called this function anything that we wanted. We chose main to be consistent with some of the other languages.

LESSON 4.3 FUNCTION ARGUMENTS

As in Lesson 4.2, parameters are the information that need to be passed to the function for it to do its work. Although parameters are also commonly referred to as arguments, arguments are thought of more as the actual values or references assigned to the parameter variables when a function is called at runtime. In simpler terms, arguments are to functions as ingredients are to a recipe.

Python supports several types of arguments, namely:

- Required arguments
- Keyword arguments
- Default arguments
- A variable number of arguments

Lesson 4.3.1 Required Arguments

Required arguments are the types of arguments that have to be present when calling a function. These types of arguments also need to be in the correct order for the function to work as expected.

Consider the following code snippet as shown in **Snippet 4.21**.

Snippet 4.21

```python
def division(first, second):
    return first/second
```

You have to pass the arguments `first` and `second` for the function to work. You also have to pass the arguments in the correct order, as switching them will yield completely different results.

You would then call the function as shown in **Snippet 4.22**.

Snippet 4.22

```python
quotient = division(10, 2)
print(quotient)
```

The result, as expected, would be as shown in **Snippet 4.23**.

Snippet 4.23

```
5.0
```

Lesson 4.3.2 Keyword Arguments

If it is necessary that you call all of the parameters in the right order, you can use keyword arguments in your function call. You can use these to identify the arguments by their parameter names. Let's consider the example from **Snippet 4.24** to make this a bit clearer.

Snippet 4.24

```python
def division(first, second):
    return first/second

quotient = division(second=2, first=10)
print(quotient)
```

As you can see, we have intentionally passed arguments in the wrong order by swapping their positions. The difference here is that we used the names of the arguments when passing them. By doing this, we corrected our *mistake,* and the function will receive its parameters in the right order and give us the correct (and expected) output, which is shown in **Snippet 4.25**.

Snippet 4.25

```
5.0
```

Keyword arguments are very powerful, and they ensure that no matter which order we pass arguments in, the function will always know which argument goes where.

Lesson 4.3.3 Default Arguments

Default arguments are those that take a default value if no argument value is passed during the function call. You can assign this default value with the assignment operator, =, just like in the example shown in **Snippet 4.26**.

Snippet 4.26

```
def division(first, second=2):
    return first/second

quotient = division(10)
print(quotient)
```

The output for this example is the same as that of the previous examples.

Note that even if the argument named second has a default value, you can still pass a value to it, and this passed value will override the default value. This means that the function will promptly ignore the default value and use whatever value you passed to it.

Snippet 4.27 is an example with the default argument where a value is passed.

Snippet 4.27

```
def division(first, second=2):
    return first/second

quotient = division(10, 5)
print(quotient)
```

As expected, the output of this code snippet is shown in **Snippet 4.28**.

Snippet 4.28

```
2.0
```

Lesson 4.3.4 Variable Number of Arguments

It might so happen that you want to allow a function to receive any number of variables, and then process them. Wouldn't it be convenient if you could pass a variable number of arguments to this function? Well, you're in luck! This is possible in Python by using the special * (asterisk) syntax.

Snippet 4.29 shows an example of using *args.

Snippet 4.29

```
def addition(*args):
    total = 0
    for i in args:
        total += i
    return total

answer = addition(20, 10, 5, 1)
print(answer)
```

Note that you don't have to name the variable *args. You could have named it *numbers, and the function would have worked just as well.

> Test yourself on this concept by completing Lab Activity 4.3: Function Arguments.

LESSON 4.4 ANONYMOUS FUNCTIONS

Anonymous functions in Python are also called **lambda functions**. This is because they use the keyword lambda in their definition.

Anonymous functions are so called because, unlike all of the other functions that we have looked at up to this point, they do not require to be named in their definition. The functions are usually throwaway, meaning that they are only required where they are defined, and are not to be called in other parts of the codebase.

The syntax of an anonymous function is shown in **Snippet 4.31**.

Snippet 4.31

```
lambda argument_list: expression
```

The argument list consists of a comma-separated list of arguments, and the expression is an arithmetic expression that uses these arguments. You can assign the function to a variable to give it a name.

> Practice this concept by completing Practice Exercise 4.4: Creating a Lambda Function.

The true power of anonymous functions can be seen when they are used in combination with the map(), reduce(), or filter() functions.

The syntax of a map() function is shown in **Snippet 4.34**.

Snippet 4.34

```
map(func, iterable)
```

The first argument, func, is the name of a function, and the second, iterable, is a sequence (for example, a list). map() applies the func function to all of the elements of the iterable sequence. It returns a new list, with the elements changed by func.

Let's suppose that you have the following list, and want to generate a new list with the squares of every item in the list:

Snippet 4.35

```
numbers = [2, 4, 6, 8, 10]
```

One way to implement this would be:

Snippet 4.36

```
numbers = [2, 4, 6, 8, 10]
squared = []

for num in numbers:
    squared.append(num**2)
```

The `for` loop, in this case, can be replaced with a lambda function that serves the same purpose, as shown in **Snippet 4.37**.

Snippet 4.37

```
lambda num: num ** 2
```

We can then use the `map()` function to apply this lambda function to each of the items in the list, in order to get their squares, as shown in **Snippet 4.38**.

Snippet 4.38

```
squared = map(lambda num: num ** 2, numbers)
```

This will yield a `map` object, and, to cast this to a list, we use the `list()` function, as shown in **Snippet 4.39**.

Snippet 4.39

```
squared = list(map(lambda num: num ** 2, numbers))
```

Our whole program then reduces to just the three lines shown in **Snippet 4.40**.

Snippet 4.40

```
numbers = [2, 4, 6, 8, 10]
squared = list(map(lambda num: num ** 2, numbers))

print(squared)
```

The output of these lines is as follows:

Snippet 4.41

```
[4, 16, 36, 64, 100]
```

This definitely shows the versatility of lambda/anonymous functions, and their ability to make our code more concise.

Test yourself on this concept by completing Lab Activity 4.4: Using Lambda Functions.

SUMMARY

In this module, we learned about the various types of functions in Python, as well as their differences, syntax, and use cases. We covered how and where to apply the different types of functions, and how they can be used to help break your programs into smaller sub-programs that achieve a specific purpose. We also saw how the use of functions can help reuse functionality in our code and avoid repeating the same blocks of code.

With this knowledge, you should be able to build all sorts of well-structured programs that will be easy to read and understand, and which will make optimal use of repetitive functionality.

In Module 5: Lists and Tuples, we will take a look at lists and tuples; it will be our first module regarding the various data structures that Python offers.

LISTS AND TUPLES

MODULE OBJECTIVES

BY THE END OF THIS MODULE, YOU WILL BE ABLE TO:

1. Create and access lists in Python
2. Describe the various methods that are available in lists, and use them in your Python programs
3. Create and access tuples in Python
4. Identify the differences between tuples and lists
5. Implement the various built-in methods that are available with tuples

INTRODUCTION

This module introduces lists and tuples in Python. We also look at the various list and tuple methods.

A **list** is a data structure that holds ordered collections of related data. Lists are known as **arrays** in other programming languages, like Java, C, and C++. Python lists, however, are more flexible and powerful than the traditional arrays of other languages.

An example of this power is that the items in a list do not have to all be of the same type. In other words, we can have a list whose items are strings, integers, or even other lists. The items in a list can be of any of the Python types.

The main properties of Python lists are as follows:

- They are ordered.
- They contain objects of arbitrary types.
- The elements of a list can be accessed by an index.
- They are arbitrarily nestable, that is, they can contain other lists as sublists.
- They have variable sizes.
- They are mutable, that is, the elements of a list can be changed.

Tuples are used to hold together multiple related objects. They are similar to the lists discussed previously, in that they are also sequence data types, but differ in that they don't have all the functionality afforded by lists. The key difference between lists and tuples is that you cannot change the elements of a tuple once they are set. This property of tuples is called **immutability**.

LESSON 5.1 LIST SYNTAX

As you saw previously, lists can be created in several ways. The simplest of them is to enclose the elements of the list in square brackets [].

In **Snippet 5.1** you can see several types of lists:

Snippet 5.1

```
# Empty list
[]

# List containing numbers
[2, 4, 6, 8, 10]

# List with mixed types
["one", 2, "three", ["five", 6]]
```

The first is an initialization of an empty list. The second is a list whose elements are numbers. The last one is an example of a list that contains several types. It has numbers, strings, and sublists inside of it.

LESSON 5.2 LIST METHODS

The list data type has some built-in methods that can be used with it. These methods are as follows:

- list.append(item)
- list.extend(iterable)
- list.insert(index, item)
- list.remove(item)
- list.pop([index])
- list.clear()
- list.index(item [, start [, end]])
- list.count(item)
- list.sort(key=None, reverse=False)
- list.reverse()
- list.copy()

Let's take a closer look at what these methods can do.

Lesson 5.2.1 list.append(item)

The list.append(item) method adds a single item to the end of a list. This doesn't return a new list – it only modifies the original. **Snippet 5.2** shows an example of this in use.

Snippet 5.2

```
>>> things = ["first"]
>>> things.append("another thing")
>>> things
['first', 'another thing']
```

Lesson 5.2.2 list.extend(iterable)

The list.extend(iterable) method takes one argument, which should be an iterable data type. It then extends the list by appending all of the items from the iterable to the list. What would happen if we would extend a list with another list? See **Snippet 5.3**.

Snippet 5.3

```
>>> things
['first', 'another thing']
>>> others = ["third", "fourth"]
>>> things.extend(others)
>>> things
['first', 'another thing', 'third', 'fourth']
```

The code in **Snippet 5.4** shows what would happen if you passed a string to the extend method.

Snippet 5.4

```
>>> things = ["first"]
>>> things.append("another thing")
>>> things['first', 'another thing']
>>> things.extend("another thing")
>>> things
['first', 'another thing', 'a', 'n', 'o', 't', 'h', 'e', 'r', ' ', 't',
'h', 'i', 'n', 'g']
```

Note that the extend method used the string as an iterable. This means that it looped through every character in the string (including the space) and appended those characters to the list.

Lesson 5.2.3 list.insert(index, item)

The list.insert(index, item) method (as the name suggests) inserts an item at a given position in a list. The method takes two arguments, index and item. The index is the position in the list before which to insert the item defined in the second argument. Both arguments are required.

Snippet 5.5 shows how to insert an item at the beginning of a list.

Snippet 5.5

```
>>> things = ["second"]
>>> things
['second']
>>> things.insert(0, "first")
>>> things
['first', 'second']
```

Lesson 5.2.4 list.remove(item)

The list.remove(item) method removes from the list the first item whose value matches the argument item that's passed in as shown in **Snippet 5.6**.

Snippet 5.6

```
>>> things = ["first", "second"]
>>> things
['first', 'second']
>>> things.remove("second")
>>> things
['first']
```

Lesson 5.2.5 list.pop([index])

The list.pop([index]) method removes the item at the given index of the list, and returns it. The index is an optional argument, and if it isn't passed in, the method will remove the last item in the list.

The code in **Snippet 5.7** shows how it works.

Snippet 5.7

```
>>> things = ["first", "second", "third"]
>>> things
['first', 'second', 'third']
>>> second_item = things.pop(1)
>>> second_item
'second'
>>> things
['first', 'third']
```

The argument that is passed in is the index of the item that you would like to pop, and not the position. Python list indices start at zero.

Lesson 5.2.6 list.clear()

As the name suggests, the list.clear() method removes all items from a list. An alternative to this method would be del list[:].

Lesson 5.2.7 list.index(item [, start [, end]])

The list.index(item [, start [, end]]) method returns the index of the first item in the list whose value is item.

The parameters start and end are optional, and they indicate the position in the list at which the search for said item should start and end, respectively. Again, the very beginning of the list is index zero. The index at the end of the list is one less than the length of the list.

To search the entire list, simply pass in the item parameter, as shown in **Snippet 5.8**.

Snippet 5.8

```
>>> things = ['first', 'second', 'third']
>>> things.index('second')
1
```

An example of where the start and end parameters are specified is shown in **Snippet 5.9**.

Snippet 5.9

```
>>> things = ['first', 'second', 'third', 'fourth']
>>> things.index('third', 1, 3)
2
```

If the specified item is not found in the list, Python raises a ValueError, as shown in **Snippet 5.10**.

Snippet 5.10

```
>>> things = ['first', 'second', 'third', 'fourth']
>>> things.index('fifth')
Traceback (most recent call last):
  File "python", line 1, in <module>
ValueError: 'fifth' is not in list
>>> things.index('fourth', 0, 2)
Traceback (most recent call last):
  File "python", line 1, in <module>
ValueError: 'fourth' is not in list
```

Lesson 5.2.8 list.count(item)

The list.count(item) method returns the number of times the given item occurs in the list.

Lesson 5.2.9 list.sort(key=None, reverse=False)

The list.sort([key=None|function, reverse=True|False]) method sorts the items of the list. The key and reverse parameters are optional. The key parameter specifies a function to be called on each list element prior to making comparisons. A common use for this is if you have a list of lists and you want to sort on an element of the sublists. If you wish to not specify a key, you can leave out this parameter or specify key = None. The reverse parameter tells the method to sort in ascending (False) or descending order (True). If this parameter is not specified, the default sort order is ascending.

Lesson 5.2.10 list.reverse()

The `list.reverse()` method reverses the elements of the list.

Lesson 5.2.11 list.copy()

The `list.copy()` method returns a shallow copy of a list. A shallow copy means that if you modify either list, the original or the copy, only that list is modified.

> Test yourself on this concept by completing Lab Activity 5.2: Using the List Methods.

LESSON 5.3 LIST COMPREHENSIONS

List comprehensions are a feature of Python that give us a clean, concise way to create lists.

A common use case would be when you need to create a list in which each element is the result of some operations applied to each member of another sequence or iterable object.

The syntax for a list comprehension is similar to creating a list the *traditional* way. It consists of square brackets [] containing an expression followed by a `for` clause, then zero or more `if` clauses.

Let's go back to the example we looked at in **Module 3: Control Statements**, where we needed to calculate the squares of numbers. To calculate the squares of all numbers from one to ten using a `for` loop, we could do what is shown in **Snippet 5.12**.

Snippet 5.12

```
>>> for num in range(1,11):
...     print(num**2)

1
4
9
16
25
36
49
64
81
100
```

The same can be achieved by using list comprehensions, as shown in **Snippet 5.13**.

Snippet 5.13

```
>>> squares = [num**2 for num in range(1, 11)]
>>> squares
[1, 4, 9, 16, 25, 36, 49, 64, 81, 100]
```

We can also use `if` statements within list comprehensions. There are really no limitations to what can be done with comprehensions. **Snippet 5.14** shows an example of the code shown in Snippet 5.13 with the addition of an `if` statement.

Snippet 5.14

```
>>> squares = [num**2 for num in range(1, 11) if num%2 == 0]
>>> squares
[4, 16, 36, 64, 100]
```

Snippet 5.14 only adds to the list those squares whose roots are even numbers.

LESSON 5.4 TUPLE SYNTAX

The main advantages of using tuples, rather than lists, are as follows:

- They are better suited for use with different (heterogeneous) data types.
- Tuples can be used as a key for a dictionary (we will see dictionaries in the next chapter). This is due to the immutable nature of tuples.
- Iterating over tuples is much faster than iterating over lists.
- They are better for passing around data that you don't want changed.

A tuple consists of a number of individual values, separated by commas (just like lists). As with lists, a tuple can contain elements of different types. You create a tuple by placing all of the comma-separated values in parentheses, `()`, as shown in **Snippet 5.15**.

Snippet 5.15

```
>>> pets = ('dog', 'cat', 'parrot')
>>> pets
('dog', 'cat', 'parrot')
>>> type(pets)
<class 'tuple'>
```

The parentheses are optional, and you might as well create a tuple using just the comma-separated values, as shown in **Snippet 5.16**.

Snippet 5.16

```
>>> pets = 'dog', 'cat', 'parrot'
>>> pets
('dog', 'cat', 'parrot')
>>> type(pets)
<class 'tuple'>
```

Note that the output version of a tuple will always be enclosed in parentheses, no matter which method you used to create it. This prevents confusion and allows us to better interpret tuples visually.

In the example of a nested tuple shown in **Snippet 5.17**, we can see why outputting in this format is important.

Snippet 5.17

```
>>> pets = ('dog', 'cat'), 'parrot'
>>> pets
(('dog', 'cat'), 'parrot')
```

Here, we can see that there is a nested tuple, (`'dog'`, `'cat'`), inside the main tuple, and the use of multiple parentheses makes this abundantly clear. This also displays another property of tuples; they can be nested with no limit. Be careful when nesting tuples, though, as several nesting levels may make it difficult to understand and navigate the structure.

What if we wanted to create a tuple with one element? We could just enclose it in parentheses, right? Consider the code shown in **Snippet 5.18**.

Snippet 5.18

```
>>> one = ('thing')
>>> one
'thing'
>>> type(one)
<class 'str'>
```

This is incorrect. As you can see in Snippet 5.18, creating a tuple in this way will only result in a string being created.

You have to recall one very important part of the definition of a tuple: It is a collection of comma-separated values. The comma is very important; therefore, you would have to do something like that shown in **Snippet 5.19** to create a tuple with one element.

Snippet 5.19

```
>>> one = 'thing',
>>> one
('thing',)
>>> type(one)
<class 'tuple'>
```

Practice this concept by completing Practice Exercise 5.4: Creating a Tuple.

LESSON 5.5 ACCESSING TUPLE ELEMENTS

Tuples give us a couple of ways to access their elements. These are as follows:

- Indexing
- Slicing

Lesson 5.5.1 Indexing

Similar to lists, we can use the index operator `[]` to access an element in a tuple by using its index. Tuple indices start at zero, just like those of lists.

Practice this concept by completing Practice Exercise 5.5A: Accessing Tuple Elements Using Indexing.

Lesson 5.5.2 Slicing

While indexing allows you to access an individual element in a tuple, slicing allows you to access a subset, or a slice, of the tuple.

Slicing uses the slicing operator, :, and the general syntax is shown in **Snippet 5.27**.

Snippet 5.27

```
tupleToSlice[Start index (included):Stop index (excluded):Increment]
```

All of these parameters are optional, and this is how they work:

- `Start index`: The index at which to start the slicing. The element at this index is included in the slice. If this parameter is absent, it is assumed to be zero, and thus, the slicing starts at the beginning of the tuple.
- `Stop index`: The index at which to stop slicing. The element at this index is not included in the slice. This means that the last item in this slice will be the one just before the stop index. If this parameter is absent, the slice ends at the very end of the tuple.
- `Increment`: This determines how many steps to take in the tuple when creating the slice. If this parameter is absent, it is assumed to be one.

Practice this concept by completing Practice Exercise 5.5B: Accessing Tuple Elements Using Slicing.

LESSON 5.6 TUPLE METHODS

Python has the following methods that work with tuples:

- `any()`: This method can be used to discover whether any element of a tuple is an iterable as shown in **Snippet 5.31**.

Snippet 5.31

```
>>> pets = ('cat', 'dog', 'horse')
>>> any(pets)
True
```

- `count()`: This method returns the number of occurrences of an item in a tuple as shown in **Snippet 5.32**. This is also the only bound method, as the syntax describes: `tuple.count(element)`.
- The other methods are unbound.

Snippet 5.32

```
>>> pets = ('cat', 'dog', 'horse')
>>> pets.count("cat")
1
```

- `min()`: This method returns the smallest element in a tuple as shown in **Snippet 5.33**.

Snippet 5.33

```
>>> pets = ('cat', 'dog', 'horse')
>>> min(pets)
'cat'
```

- `max()`: This method returns the largest element in a tuple as shown in **Snippet 5.34**.

Snippet 5.34

```
>>> pets = ('cat', 'dog', 'horse')
>>> max(pets)
'horse'
```

- `len()`: This method returns the total number of elements in a tuple as shown in **Snippet 5.35**.

Snippet 5.35

```
>>> pets = ('cat', 'dog', 'horse')
>>> len(pets)
3
```

- Tuples, just like strings, can be concatenated. This is shown in **Snippet 5.36**.

Snippet 5.36

```
>>> pets = ('cat', 'dog', 'horse')
>>> wild = ('lion', 'zebra', 'antelope')
>>> animals = pets + wild
>>> print(animals)
('cat', 'dog', 'horse', 'lion', 'zebra', 'antelope')
```

Test yourself on this concept by completing Lab Activity 5.6: Using Tuple Methods.

SUMMARY

In this module, we expanded our knowledge on Python lists. We have looked at the various methods that are available for lists, and how to use them in practical applications. We have also seen how we can use list comprehensions to make the task of building lists programmatically easier.

Next, we covered Python tuples. We looked at the various methods that are available for tuple operations, and how to use them in practical applications. We have also seen how we can access tuple elements.

In the next module, **Module 6: Dictionaries and Sets**, we will cover sets and dictionaries, which are the other data structures that Python offers.

DICTIONARIES AND SETS

MODULE OBJECTIVES

BY THE END OF THIS MODULE, YOU WILL BE ABLE TO:

1. Create and use dictionaries
2. Use methods and attributes associated with dictionaries
3. Describe and use ordered dictionaries to store and retrieve data in a predictable order
4. Create sets, as well as add, read, and remove data from them
5. Describe the attributes defined on set objects
6. Describe frozen sets

INTRODUCTION

This module describes dictionaries and sets. We cover creating, reading, and writing data to these data structures.

You have already seen lists that hold values that you can access by using indexes. However, what if you wanted to name each value, instead of using an index? For example, suppose that you want to access a list of cake ingredients, but you do not know where that list resides in the array. In that case, a dictionary would come in handy.

Dictionaries, sometimes referred to as associative arrays in other languages, are data structures that hold data or information in a key-value order. Dictionaries allow you to access whatever value you want, using the much easier to remember key.

Dictionaries, unlike lists, are indexed using keys, which are usually strings. There are two kinds of dictionaries that you can use in Python: The default `dict`, which is unordered, and a special kind of dictionary called an `OrderedDict`. The difference is that the keys in the default dictionary are stored in an unordered manner, whereas an `OrderedDict` stores key-value pairs in the order of insertion.

A **set** is a collection of data items that are unordered and unique, that is, items cannot be repeated. For example, [1, 1] is a valid list, but not a valid set. With no duplicates in sets, we are able to perform mathematical operations, such as unions and intersection. You can store any kind of valid string or integer in a set, as long as it is unique.

For background information, sets are very important objects in mathematics, as well. A whole branch of mathematics, called *set theory*, has been dedicated to the study of sets and their properties. We will not get into a lot of the mathematics around sets, but we will discuss some basic set operations.

Suppose that we have a set, $A = \{1,2,3\}$, and another set, $B = \{3,4,5\}$.

The **union** of set A and B, mathematically denoted as $A \cup B$, will be $\{1,2,3,4,5\}$. The union is simply the set of everything in A and B. Remember, there are no duplicates, so 3 will appear only once.

On the other hand, the **intersection** of A and B, denoted as $A \cap B$, will be the set of everything that is common in both A and B, which, in our case, is just $\{3\}$.

LESSON 6.1 WORKING WITH DICTIONARIES

You can create a dictionary in two ways. The first way is to simply assign an empty dictionary to a variable by using curly brackets, as shown in **Snippet 6.1**.

Snippet 6.1

```
dictionary = {}
```

The second way is to use the dict () function to return a new dictionary, as shown in **Snippet 6.2**.

Snippet 6.2

```
dictionary = dict()
```

In both cases, a dictionary object will be created. We can inspect the attributes and properties defined on the dictionary object by using the built-in dir () function, as shown in **Snippet 6.3**.

Snippet 6.3

```
>>> dir(dictionary)
['__class__', '__contains__', '__delattr__', '__delitem__', '__dir__',
'__doc__', '__eq__', '__format__', '__ge__', '__getattribute__',
'__getitem__', '__gt__', '__hash__', '__init__', '__init_subclass__',
'__iter__', '__le__', '__len__', '__lt__', '__ne__', '__new__',
'__reduce__', '__reduce_ex__', '__repr__', '__setattr__', '__setitem__',
'__sizeof__', '__str__', '__subclasshook__', 'clear', 'copy', 'fromkeys',
'get', 'items', 'keys', 'pop', 'popitem', 'setdefault', 'update', 'values']
```

We can also confirm that we have an actual dictionary by using the built-in `isinstance()` function to check that `dictionary` is an instance of the `dict` class, as shown in **Snippet 6.4**.

Snippet 6.4

```
>>> isinstance(dictionary, dict)
True
```

The `isinstance()` function is used to check the type of an object. It takes two arguments, the first one being the object being inspected, and the second being the class that we want to type-check against; for example, `int`, `str`, `dict`, `list`, and so on.

Test yourself on this concept by completing Lab Activity 6.1A: Creating a Dictionary.

Lesson 6.1.1 Adding Data to a Dictionary

Consider the code shown in **Snippet 6.6**. In it, we add data to a dictionary during its creation by using the `dict` function and curly bracket notation.

Snippet 6.6

```
dictionary1 = dict(
    state="NY",
    city="New York"
)

print(dictionary1)

dictionary2 = {
    "state": "Maryland",
    "city": "Baltimore"
}

print(dictionary2)
```

Notice that when we use the `dict()` function, we assign values to keys using the = operator. When using { }, we separate the keys (which are strings) from the values by using :. Running the code in Snippet 6.6 will print the output shown in **Snippet 6.7**.

Snippet 6.7

```
{'state': 'NY', 'city': 'New York'}
{'state': 'Maryland', 'city': 'Baltimore'}
```

We assign values to existing dictionaries using keys as shown in **Snippet 6.8**.

Snippet 6.8

```
>>> dictionary2['bird'] = 'Baltimore oriole'
```

As **Snippet 6.9** shows, this will add a new key to `dictionary2`, with the name `bird` and the value `Baltimore oriole`.

Snippet 6.9

```
>>> print(dictionary2)
{'state': 'Maryland', 'city': 'Baltimore', 'bird': 'Baltimore
oriole'}
```

On the other hand, using the preceding format with an existing key will reassign that key to a new value. **Snippet 6.10** demonstrates how to assign a new value to the key `state` of `dictionary1`.

Snippet 6.10

```
>>> dictionary1['state'] = 'New York'
```

This will change the value of `state` from `NY` to `New York`, as shown in **Snippet 6.11**.

Snippet 6.11

```
>>> print(dictionary1)
{'state': 'New York', 'city': 'New York'}
```

Lesson 6.1.2 Reading Data from a Dictionary

To read data from a dictionary, you can access dictionary values via their keys, as shown in **Snippet 6.12**.

Snippet 6.12

```
>>>print(dictionary1['state'])
New York
```

Using this format, if the key does not exist, we will get a `KeyError`. **Snippet 6.13** shows an example of this error.

Snippet 6.13

```
>>> print(dictionary1['age'])
Traceback (most recent call last):
  File "python", line 1, in <module>
KeyError: 'age'
```

To avoid this error, we can also access values from dictionaries by using their get() function.

The `get()` function returns `None` if an item does not exist. You can also use the `get()` function to specify what should be returned when no value exists. Use the `get()` function, as shown in **Snippet 6.14**.

Snippet 6.14

```
print(dictionary1.get('state'))
print(dictionary1.get('age'))
print(dictionary1.get('age', 'Key age is not defined'))
```

The code in **Snippet 6.14** will result in the output shown in **Snippet 6.15**.

Snippet 6.15

```
New York
None
Key age is not defined
```

Lesson 6.1.3 Iterating through Dictionaries

The simplest way to iterate through dictionaries is to use a `for` loop. Consider the script shown in **Snippet 6.16**. The script uses a `for` loop, in order to get the dictionary's keys.

Snippet 6.16

```
dictionary1 = dict(
    state="NY",
    city="New York"
)

for item in dictionary1:
    print(item)
```

The code shown in **Snippet 6.16**, by default, iterates through the dictionary's keys, and will print the output shown in **Snippet 6.17**.

Snippet 6.17

```
state
city
```

You can also explicitly iterate through only the keys or the values of a dictionary by calling the `keys()` method, which returns a list of keys, or the `values()` method, which returns a list of values in the dictionary. Use the `keys()` method as shown in the script in **Snippet 6.18**.

Snippet 6.18

```
dictionary1 = dict(
    state="NY",
    city="New York"
)

for item in dictionary1.keys():
    print(item)
```

Snippet 6.18 will print the output shown in **Snippet 6.19**. You will see this matches the output shown in Snippet 6.17.

Snippet 6.19

```
state
city
```

Use the `values()` method as shown in the script in **Snippet 6.20**, in order to print the values.

Snippet 6.20

```
dictionary1 = dict(
    state="NY",
    city="New York"
)

for item in dictionary1.values():
    print(item)
```

The output for the script in Snippet 6.20 is shown in **Snippet 6.21**.

Snippet 6.21

```
NY
New York
```

You can also iterate through both keys and values at the same time using the `items()` method. Use a `for` loop, as shown in the script in **Snippet 6.22**, in order to print both keys and values.

Snippet 6.22

```
dictionary1 = dict(
    state="NY",
    city="New York"
)


for key, value in dictionary1.items():
    print(key, value)
```

Snippet 6.22 will print the output shown in **Snippet 6.23**.

Snippet 6.23

```
state NY
city New York
```

Practice this concept by completing Practice Exercise 6.1: Adding, Reading, and Iterating through a Dictionary.

Lesson 6.1.4 Checking for the Existence of Particular Keys

You can use the `in` keyword to check whether a particular key exists in a dictionary, without iterating through it. This works the same way as it does in lists, and you will get back a Boolean value of `True` if the key exists, and `False` if it doesn't. Consider the script in **Snippet 6.44**.

Snippet 6.44

```
a = {
    "size": "10 feet",
    "weight": "16 pounds"
}

print("size" in a)
print("length" in a)
```

The example in Snippet 6.44 will print the output shown in **Snippet 6.45**.

Snippet 6.45

```
True
False
```

Test yourself on this concept by completing Lab Activity 6.1B: Arranging and Presenting Data Using Dictionaries.

Test yourself on this concept by completing Lab Activity 6.1C: Combining Dictionaries.

LESSON 6.2 ADDITIONAL DICTIONARY ATTRIBUTES

If you run the `dir()` function on a dictionary, you will see a few more attributes defined that we have not yet touched upon. **Snippet 6.48** shows a sample output.

Snippet 6.48

```
['__class__', '__contains__', '__delattr__', '__delitem__', '__dir__',
'__doc__', '__eq__', '__format__', '__ge__', '__getattribute__',
'__getitem__', '__gt__', '__hash__', '__init__', '__init_subclass__',
'__iter__', '__le__', '__len__', '__lt__', '__ne__', '__new__',
'__reduce__', '__reduce_ex__', '__repr__', '__setattr__', '__setitem__',
'__sizeof__', '__str__', '__subclasshook__', 'clear', 'copy', 'fromkeys',
'get', 'items', 'keys', 'pop', 'popitem', 'setdefault', 'update', 'values']
```

Let's go through some of these attributes and see what they can do.

Lesson 6.2.1 dict.update()

The `update()` method on dictionaries is used to insert new key-value pairs into a dictionary, or update the value of an existing one.

For example, if we have an empty dictionary, calling update() will insert a new entry as shown in **Snippet 6.49**.

Snippet 6.49

```
>>> a = {}
>>> a.update({"name": "Dan Brown"})
>>> a
{'name': 'Dan Brown'}
```

What if we update the name key again? Consider the code shown in **Snippet 6.50**.

Snippet 6.50

```
>>> a.update({"name": "Dan Brown Xavier"})
>>> a
{'name': 'Dan Brown Xavier'}
```

As you can see, calling .update() with an existing key replaces the value of that key. Also, note that the .update() function takes a dictionary with the key-value pairs defined, in order to update the existing dictionary. This means that the .update() function would come in handy if you had two dictionaries with different keys that you wanted to combine into one.

Lesson 6.2.2 dict.clear() and dict.pop()

The clear() method is used to remove all keys from a dictionary. Consider the example in **Snippet 6.51**.

Snippet 6.51

```
>>> a
{'name': 'Dan Brown Xavier'}
>>> a.clear()
>>> a
{}
```

If you only want to remove one key-value pair, you can use the del keyword, as shown in **Snippet 6.52**.

Snippet 6.52

```
>>> a = {"name": "Skandar Keynes", "age": "24"}
>>> del a["name"]
>>> a
{'age': '24'}
```

What if you want to remove a key-value pair from the dictionary and do something with the value? In that case, you can use pop(), which will delete the entry from the dictionary and return the value as shown in **Snippet 6.53**.

Snippet 6.53

```
>>> a = {"name": "Skandar Keynes", "age": "24"}
>>> b = a.pop("name")
>>> a
{'age': '24'}
>>> b
'Skandar Keynes'
```

Lesson 6.2.3 dict.copy()

The copy() method is used to create shallow copies of dictionaries, as shown in **Snippet 6.54**.

Snippet 6.54

```
>>> a = {"name": "Skandar Keynes", "age": "24"}
>>> b = a.copy()
>>> b
{'name': 'Skandar Keynes', 'age': '24'}
>>> a["name"] = "Janet Jackson"
>>> a
{'name': 'Janet Jackson', 'age': '24'}
>>> b
{'name': 'Skandar Keynes', 'age': '24'}
```

In the example shown in Snippet 6.54, you can see that b is a **shallow copy** of a, and has all of the exact key-value pairs found in a. However, updating a will not update b. They exist as two different entities.

This is different from using the = operator to make a **deep copy**, where a and b will refer to the same object, and updating one will update the other. Consider **Snippet 6.55**.

Snippet 6.55

```
>>> a = {"name": "Skandar Keynes", "age": "24"}
>>> b = a
>>> a["name"] = "Janet Jackson"
>>> b["age"] = 16
>>> a
{'name': 'Janet Jackson', 'age': 16}
>>> b
{'name': 'Janet Jackson', 'age': 16}
```

Lesson 6.2.4 dict.popitem()

The popitem() method pops and returns a random item from the dictionary. That item will no longer exist in the dictionary after that. For an example, see **Snippet 6.56**.

Snippet 6.56

```
>>> a = {"name": "Skandar Keynes", "age": "24", "sex": "male"}
>>> a.popitem()
('sex', 'male')
>>> a.popitem()
('age', '24')
>>> a
{'name': 'Skandar Keynes'}
```

Lesson 6.2.5 dict.setdefault()

The `setdefault()` method takes two arguments: a key to be searched for in the dictionary, and a value. If the key exists in the dictionary, its value will be returned. If the key does not exist, it will be inserted with the value provided in the second argument. If no second argument was passed, any insertion will be done with the value `None`.

Snippet 6.57 shows an example where the key exists in the dictionary.

Snippet 6.57

```
>>> a = {"name": "Skandar Keynes", "age": "24", "sex": "male"}
>>> b = a.setdefault("name")
>>> a
{'name': 'Skandar Keynes', 'age': '24', 'sex': 'male'}
>>> b
'Skandar Keynes'
```

In this case, the value is returned as is, and the dictionary is left untouched. Passing the second argument in this case will have no effect, because a value already exists.

Snippet 6.58 shows another example, in which the key does not exist in the dictionary, and a value was passed. In this case, the key-value pair will be added to the dictionary, and the value will be returned, as well.

Snippet 6.58

```
>>> a = {"name": "Skandar Keynes", "age": "24", "sex": "male"}
>>> b = a.setdefault("planet", "Earth")
>>> a
{'name': 'Skandar Keynes', 'age': '24', 'sex': 'male', 'planet': 'Earth'}
>>> b
'Earth'
```

Now, let's look at a final example in **Snippet 6.59**, in which the key does not exist in the dictionary, and no value was passed. In this case, the key will be added with a value of `None`. Nothing will be returned.

Snippet 6.59

```
>>> a = {"name": "Skandar Keynes", "age": "24", "sex": "male"}
>>> b = a.setdefault("planet")
>>> a
{'name': 'Skandar Keynes', 'age': '24', 'sex': 'male', 'planet': None}
>>> b
>>>
```

Lesson 6.2.6 dict.fromkeys()

The `fromkeys()` method is used to create a dictionary from an iterable of keys, with whatever value is provided by the user. An iterable is anything that you can iterate over (for example, using a `for` loop).

Snippet 6.60 shows an example of this.

Snippet 6.60

```
>>> a = dict.fromkeys(["name", "age"], "Nothing here yet")
>>> a
{'name': 'Nothing here yet', 'age': 'Nothing here yet'}
```

Note that if you do not provide a second argument, the values will be auto-set to None as shown in **Snippet 6.61**.

Snippet 6.61

```
>>> a = dict.fromkeys(["name", "age"])
>>> a
{'name': None, 'age': None}
```

Practice this concept by completing Practice Exercise 6.2: Updating, Editing, and Copying from a Dictionary.

LESSON 6.3 ORDERED DICTIONARIES

So far, the dictionaries that we have created do not maintain the insertion order of the key-value pairs that are added. **Ordered dictionaries** are dictionaries that maintain the insertion order of keys. This means that when you are iterating through them, you will always access the keys in the order in which they were inserted.

The OrderedDict class is a dict subclass defined in the collections package that Python ships with. We will use ordered dictionaries when it is vitally important to store and retrieve data in a predictable order; for example, when reading database entries.

Creating an ordered dictionary is as easy as creating an instance of the OrderedDict class and passing in key-value pairs as shown in **Snippet 6.78**.

Snippet 6.78

```
>>> from collections import OrderedDict
>>> a = OrderedDict(name="Zeus", role="god")
>>> a
OrderedDict([('name', 'Zeus'), ('role', 'god')])
```

Everything about OrderedDict, except for it maintaining an internal key order, is similar to normal dictionaries. However, if you inspect the attributes defined on it using dir(), you may see some new ones that were not in the normal dict() class that we looked at previously as shown in **Snippet 6.79**.

Snippet 6.79

```
['__class__', '__contains__', '__delattr__', '__delitem__', '__dict__',
'__dir__', '__doc__', '__eq__', '__format__', '__ge__', __getattribute__',
'__getitem__', '__gt__', '__hash__', '__init__', '__init_subclass__',
'__iter__', '__le__', '__len__', '__lt__', '__ne__', '__new__',
'__reduce__', '__reduce_ex__', '__repr__', '__reversed__', '__setattr__',
'__setitem__', '__sizeof__', '__str__', '__subclasshook__', 'clear',
'copy', 'fromkeys', 'get', 'items', 'keys', 'move_to_end', 'pop',
'popitem', 'setdefault', 'update', 'values']
```

One of the new attributes is move to end, which moves a key contained in the OrderedDict from its current position to the very end of the dictionary.

Note that when you are checking whether two `OrderedDict` are equal, the order of keys is also considered. Although for a normal `dict`, having the same key-value pairs is enough to declare equality, in `OrderedDict`, if they are not in the same order, those two objects are not equal.

LESSON 6.4 THE BASICS OF SETS

In this lesson, we are going to cover sets, which are unique data structures with interesting properties. Remember that a set is a collection of data items that are unordered and unique.

Let's begin our journey into sets by looking at how to create sets, how to read data from them, and how to remove data from them.

Lesson 6.4.1 Creating Sets

You can create a set in two ways. The first way to create a set is to use the built-in `set` function. The function takes either an iterable (such as a list or a tuple) or a sequence (lists, tuples, and strings are all sequences). **Snippet 6.80** shows how to use the `set` function to define the sets named a and b.

Snippet 6.80

```
>>> a = set([1,2,3])
>>> a
{1, 2, 3}
>>> b = set((1,2,2,3,4))
>>> b
{1, 2, 3, 4}
```

Note that in set b, all duplicated values in the original tuple were dropped.

Another way is to use the curly bracket notation. Create a set directly, by using the curly bracket notation, as shown in **Snippet 6.81**.

Snippet 6.81

```
>>> c = {'a', 'b', 'c'}
>>> c
{'b', 'a', 'c'}
```

Snippet 6.82 demonstrates how to pass a sequence to the `set()` function. As you can see, this builds a set of the sequence's constituent elements.

Snippet 6.82

```
>>> a = set("A random string")
>>> a
{'d', 'g', 's', 'A', 't', ' ', 'r', 'm', 'o', 'i', 'n', 'a'}
```

NOTE   Passing a dictionary to the set() method will create a set of its keys.

Inspect the set by using the dir() function; you should see output similar to **Snippet 6.83**.

Snippet 6.83

```
['__and__', '__class__', '__contains__', '__delattr__', '__dir__',
 '__doc__', '__eq__', '__format__', '__ge__', '__getattribute__',
 '__gt__', '__hash__', '__iand__', '__init__', '__init_subclass__',
 '__ior__', '__isub__', '__iter__', '__ixor__', '__le__', '__len__',
 '__lt__', '__ne__', '__new__', '__or__', '__rand__', '__reduce__',
 '__reduce_ex__', '__repr__', '__ror__', '__rsub__', '__rxor__',
 '__setattr__', '__sizeof__', '__str__', '__sub__',
 '__subclasshook__', '__xor__', 'add', 'clear', 'copy', 'difference',
 'difference_update', 'discard', 'intersection',
 'intersection_update', 'isdisjoint', 'issubset', 'issuperset', 'pop',
 'remove', 'symmetric_difference', 'symmetric_difference_update',
 'union', 'update']
```

We will look at some of the attributes defined on the set object later in this module.

Lesson 6.4.2 Adding Data to a Set

We add data to a set by using the set.add() and update() methods.

Add data to an existing set by using the set.add() method as shown in **Snippet 6.84**.

Snippet 6.84

```
>>> a = {1,2,3}
>>> a
{1, 2, 3}
>>> a.add(4)
>>> a
{1, 2, 3, 4}
```

Of course, because this is a set, adding a value more than once will not change the set. The item will only appear once. Add 4 to set a again, in order to verify this as shown in **Snippet 6.85**.

Snippet 6.85

```
>>> a
{1, 2, 3, 4}
>>> a.add(4)
>>> a
{1, 2, 3, 4}
```

You can also use the **set's** update() method to add items to the set, by using iterables. Use the update() method to pass in a list of values, as shown in **Snippet 6.86**.

Snippet 6.86

```
>>> a = {1,2,3}
>>> a
{1, 2, 3}
>>> a.update([3,4,5,6])
>>> a
{1, 2, 3, 4, 5, 6}
```

Lesson 6.4.3 Reading Data from a Set

Set objects do not support indexes, so you cannot access values from them using indexes, like you can in a list or a tuple.

One way to read data from a set is to iterate through the set using a for loop, as shown in **Snippet 6.87**.

Snippet 6.87

```
a = {1,2,3,4}

for num in a:
    print(num)
```

The code in Snippet 6.87 will print the output shown in **Snippet 6.88**.

Snippet 6.88

```
1
2
3
4
```

Another way to read a set's data is to use the set's pop() method to remove and return an item from the set. Items are removed from the beginning of the set, as demonstrated in **Snippet 6.89**.

Snippet 6.89

```
>>> a
{1, 2, 3, 4}
>>> a.pop()
1
>>> a
{2, 3, 4}
>>> a.pop()
2
>>> a
{3, 4}
```

Sets have more utility in the actions that we can perform on them than as a storage of data. This means that finding things like the union and intersection of items in sets gives us more insight into the data they hold.

Test yourself on this concept by completing Lab Activity 6.4: Building a Set.

Lesson 6.4.4 Removing Data from a Set

There are other ways to remove data from sets without using pop(), especially if you just want to remove the data and not return it.

One way is to use the remove() method, as shown in **Snippet 6.91**.

Snippet 6.91

```
>>> a = {1,2,3}
>>> a.remove(3)
>>> a
{1, 2}
```

As you can see, remove() drops the item from the set and does not return it. If you try to remove a non-existing item, a KeyError will be raised. For set a, remove the value 3 as shown in **Snippet 6.92**.

Snippet 6.92

```
>>> a
{1, 2}
>>> a.remove(3)
Traceback (most recent call last):
  File "<input>", line 1, in <module>
>>> a.remove(3)
KeyError: 3
```

You can also use the discard() method. For comparison, discard() does not raise a KeyError if the item to be discarded does not exist. Use the discard method, as shown in **Snippet 6.93**.

Snippet 6.93

```
>>> a = {1,2,3}
>>> a.discard(2)
>>> a
{1, 3}
>>> a.discard("nonexistent item")
>>> a
{1, 3}
```

Lastly, use the clear() method to remove all of the data from the set object as shown in **Snippet 6.94**.

Snippet 6.94

```
>>> a = {1,2,3,4,5,6}
>>> a
{1, 2, 3, 4, 5, 6}
>>> a.clear()
>>> a
set()
```

Practice this concept by completing Practice Exercise 6.4: Adding, Reading, Editing, and Building a Set.

LESSON 6.5 SET OPERATIONS

In this lesson, we will look at all of the different operations we can perform on a set.

Lesson 6.5.1 Union

As we stated earlier, a union between sets is the set of all items/elements in both sets. A union can be represented by the Venn diagram shown in **Figure 6.1**.

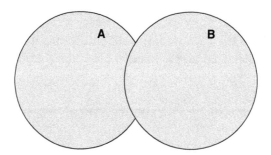

Figure 6.1   Union of sets A and B

For example, if set A = {1,2,3,4,5,6} and set B = {1,2,3,7,8,9,10}, then $A \cup B$ will be {1,2,3,4,5,6,7,8,9,10}.

To achieve union between sets in Python, we can use the union method, which is defined on set objects. An example is shown in **Snippet 6.107**.

Snippet 6.107

```
>>> a = {1,2,3,4,5,6}
>>> b = {1,2,3,7,8,9,10}
>>> a.union(b)
{1, 2, 3, 4, 5, 6, 7, 8, 9, 10}
>>> b.union(a)
{1, 2, 3, 4, 5, 6, 7, 8, 9, 10}
```

Another way to achieve union between sets in Python is to use the | operator as shown in **Snippet 6.108**.

Snippet 6.108

```
>>> a = {1,2,3,4,5,6}
>>> b = {1,2,3,7,8,9,10}
>>> a | b
{1, 2, 3, 4, 5, 6, 7, 8, 9, 10}
```

Test yourself on this concept by completing Lab Activity 6.5: Creating Unions of Elements in a Collection.

Lesson 6.5.2 Intersection

An intersection of sets is the set of all items that appear in all of the sets, that is, what they have in common. An intersection can be represented by the Venn diagram shown in **Figure 6.2**, with the dark purple area being the intersection:

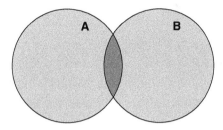

Figure 6.2   Intersection of sets A and B

As in our previous example, if set $A = \{1,2,3,4,5,6\}$ and set $B = \{1,2,3,7,8,9,10\}$, then $A \cap B$ will be $\{1,2,3\}$.

To find the intersection between sets, we can use the `intersection` method, which is defined on set objects. An example is shown in **Snippet 6.110**.

Snippet 6.110

```
>>> a = {1,2,3,4,5,6}
>>> b = {1,2,3,7,8,9,10}
>>> a.intersection(b)
{1, 2, 3}
>>> b.intersection(a)
{1, 2, 3}
```

To find the intersection between sets, you can also use the & operator as shown in **Snippet 6.111**.

Snippet 6.111

```
>>> a = {1,2,3,4,5,6}
>>> b = {1,2,3,7,8,9,10}
>>> a & b
{1, 2, 3}
```

Lesson 6.5.3 Difference

The difference between two sets is basically what is in one set and not in the other.

If set $A = \{1,2,3,4,5,6\}$ and set $B = \{1,2,3,7,8,9,10\}$, $A - B$ will be the set of items that are only in A, that is, $\{4,5,6\}$. Similarly, $B - A$ will be the set $\{7,8,9,10\}$.

The diagram shown in **Figure 6.3** illustrates $A - B$.

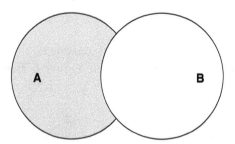

Figure 6.3   Difference of sets A
and B (A − B)

Programmatically, in Python, we can use the − operator or the `difference()` method, as shown in **Snippet 6.112**.

Snippet 6.112

```
>>> a = {1,2,3,4,5,6}
>>> b = {1,2,3,7,8,9,10}
>>> a - b
{4, 5, 6}
>>> b - a
{7, 8, 9, 10, }
>>> a.difference(b)
{4, 5, 6}
>>> b.difference(a)
{8, 9, 10, 7}
```

You can also get the **symmetric difference** between sets, which is the set of everything that is not in the intersection of the sets, as shown in **Snippet 6.113**.

Snippet 6.113

```
>>> a = {1,2,3,4,5,6}
>>> b = {1,2,3,7,8,9,10}
>>> a.symmetric_difference(b)
{4, 5, 6, 7, 8, 9, 10}
```

Lesson 6.5.4 Subsets

The `issubset()` method can be used to check whether all of one set's elements exist in another set (that is, whether the set is a subset of another). An example is shown in **Snippet 6.114**.

Snippet 6.114

```
>>> a = {1,2,3,4,5,6,7,8,9,10}
>>> b = {5,2,10}
>>> a.issubset(b)
False
>>> b.issubset(a)
True
```

In the example shown in Snippet 6.114, all of the elements in b are a small part of what is in a. Therefore, b is a subset of a. We call a a superset of b; see **Snippet 6.115**.

Snippet 6.115

```
>>> a.issuperset(b)
True
```

Lesson 6.5.5 Equality

You can check whether the two sets are equivalent by using the == operator, and whether they are not equivalent by using the != operator.

See **Snippet 6.116** for an example.

Snippet 6.116

```
>>> a = {1,2,3}
>>> b = a.copy()
>>> c = {"money", "fame"}
>>> a == b
True
>>> a == c
False
>>> c != a
True
```

> **NOTE** The copy() method, as used on sets, produces a shallow copy of a set, much like the dictionary's copy method. A shallow copy means that only references to values are copied, not the values themselves.

Lesson 6.5.6 Update Methods

You can update a set with values from the results of set operations by using the special update operations defined on the set.

These methods are as follows:

- difference_update(): This method removes all of the values of the other set from the set it is called on, as shown in **Snippet 6.117**.

Snippet 6.117

```
>>> a = {1,2,3}
>>> b = {3,4,5}
>>> a - b
{1, 2}
>>> a.difference_update(b)
>>> a
{1, 2}
```

- `intersection_update()`: This method updates the set it is called on with the intersection of itself and another set that is passed as an argument, as shown in **Snippet 6.118**.

Snippet 6.118

```
>>> a = {1,2,3}
>>> b = {3,4,5}
>>> a.intersection(b)
{3}
>>> a.intersection_update(b)
>>> a
{3}
```

- `symmetric_difference_update()`: This method updates a set that it is called on with the symmetric difference between it and the set passed as an argument, as shown in **Snippet 6.119**.

Snippet 6.119

```
>>> a = {1,2,3}
>>> b = {3,4,5}
>>> a.symmetric_difference(b)
{1, 2, 4, 5}
>>> a.symmetric_difference_update(b)
>>> a
{1, 2, 4, 5}
```

Practice this concept by completing Practice Exercise 6.5: Unions, Differences, and Intersections of Sets.

LESSON 6.6 FROZEN SETS

Frozen sets are just like sets, and they support all other set operations. However, they are immutable, and they do not support adding or removing items. Frozen sets are useful for holding items that do not need to change; for example, a set containing the names of states in the United States.

To create a frozen set, you can call the built-in `frozenset()` function with an iterable, as shown in **Snippet 6.129**.

Snippet 6.129

```
>>> a = frozenset([1,2,3])
>>> a
frozenset({1, 2, 3})
>>> dir(a)
['__and__', '__class__', '__contains__', '__delattr__', '__dir__',
'__doc__', '__eq__', '__format__', '__ge__', '__getattribute__',
'__gt__', '__hash__', '__init__', '__init_subclass__', '__iter__',
'__le__', '__len__', '__lt__', '__ne__', '__new__', '__or__',
'__rand__', '__reduce__', '__reduce_ex__', '__repr__', '__ror__',
'__rsub__', '__rxor__', '__setattr__', '__sizeof__', '__str__',
'__sub__', '__subclasshook__', '__xor__', 'copy', 'difference',
'intersection', 'isdisjoint', 'issubset', 'issuperset',
'symmetric_difference', 'union']
```

As you can see from the output of `dir()`, the `add`, `update`, `pop`, `discard`, and other methods that modify the structure of the frozen set are not defined.

> Practice this concept by completing Practice Exercise 6.6: Frozen Sets.

SUMMARY

In this module, we covered dictionaries and their types (the default, unordered `dict`, and the specialized `OrderedDict`). We also looked at attributes defined on dictionary objects and their use cases; for example, `update()` and `setdefault()`. Using these attributes, we learned how to iterate through dictionaries and modify them to achieve particular goals.

We also covered sets in this module, which are collections of unique and unordered items. We covered operations that you can perform on sets, such as finding unions and intersections, and other specialized operations, such as finding the difference and symmetric difference. We also looked at frozen sets and the potential uses for them.

In the next module, **Module 7: Object-Oriented Programming**, we will begin our journey into object-oriented programming (OOP) with Python, and we will look at how Python implements OOP concepts, such as classes and inheritance.

OBJECT-ORIENTED PROGRAMMING

MODULE OBJECTIVES

BY THE END OF THIS MODULE, YOU WILL BE ABLE TO:

1. Explain different OOP concepts and the importance of OOP

2. Instantiate a class

3. Describe how to define instance methods and pass arguments to them

4. Declare class attributes and class methods

5. Describe how to override methods

6. Implement multiple inheritance

INTRODUCTION

This module introduces object-oriented programming as implemented in Python. We also cover classes and methods, as well as overriding methods and inheritance.

A programming paradigm is a style of reasoning about programming problems. Problems, in general, can often be solved in multiple ways; for example, to calculate the sum of 2 and 3, you can use a calculator, you can use your fingers, you can use a tally mark, and so on. Similarly, in programming, you can solve problems in different ways.

At the beginning of this course, we mentioned that Python is multi-paradigm, as it supports solving problems in a functional, imperative, procedural, and object-oriented way. In this module, we will be diving into object-oriented programming in Python.

LESSON 7.1 A FIRST LOOK AT OOP

Object-oriented Programming (OOP) is a programming paradigm based on the concept of objects. Objects can be thought of as capsules of properties and procedures/methods. In an interview with *Rolling Stone* magazine, Steve Jobs, co-founder of Apple, once explained OOP in the following way:

> *"Objects are like people. They're living, breathing things that have knowledge inside them about how to do things and have memory inside them so that they can remember things. And rather than interacting with them at a very low level, you interact with them at a very high level of abstraction..."*

> **Steve Jobs**; *Rolling Stone; June 16, 1994*

An example of an object you can consider is a car. A car has multiple different attributes. It has a number of doors, a color, and a transmission type (manual or automatic). A car, regardless of the type, also has specific actions or behaviors: It can start, accelerate, decelerate, and change gears. Regardless of how these behaviors are implemented, the only thing we, the users of the car, care about is that the aforementioned behaviors, such as acceleration, actually work.

In OOP, reasoning about data as objects allows us to abstract the actual code and think more about the attributes of the data and the operations around the data. OOP offers the following advantages:

- It makes code reusable.
- It makes it easier to design software as you can model it in terms of real-world objects.
- It makes it easier to test, debug, and maintain.
- The data is secure due to abstraction and data hiding.

With the benefits it confers, OOP is a powerful tool in a programmer's tool box. In the next lesson, we will be looking at how OOP is used in Python.

LESSON 7.2 OOP IN PYTHON

Classes are a fundamental building block of object-oriented programming. They can be likened to blueprints for an object, as they define what properties and methods/behaviors an object should have.

For example, when building a house, you would follow a blueprint that tells you things such as how many rooms the house has, where the rooms are positioned relative to one another, or how the plumbing and electrical circuitry is laid out. In OOP, this building blueprint would be the class, while the house would be the instance/object.

In the earlier modules, we mentioned that everything in Python is an object. Every data type and data structure you have encountered thus far, from lists and strings to integers, functions, and others, are objects. This is why when we run the type function on any object, it will have output similar to that shown in **Snippet 7.1**.

Snippet 7.1

```
>>> type([1, 2, 3])
<class 'list'>
>>> type("foobar")
<class 'str'>
>>> type({"a": 1, "b": 2})
<class 'dict'>
>>> def func(): return True
...
>>> type(func)
<class 'function'>
>>>
```

You will note that calling the type function on each object prints out that it is an instance of a specific class. Lists are instances of the list class, strings are instances of the str class, dictionaries are instances of the dict class, and so on and so forth.

Each class is a blueprint that defines what behaviors and attributes objects will contain and how they will behave; for example, all of the lists that you create will have the lists.append method, which allows you to add elements to the list.

In **Snippet 7.2** we are creating an instance of the list class and printing out the append and remove methods. It tells us that they are methods of the list object we have instantiated.

Snippet 7.2

```
>>> l = [1, 2, 3, 4, 5] # create a list object
>>> print(l.append)
<built-in method append of list object at 0x10dd36a08>
>>> print(l.remove)
<built-in method remove of list object at 0x10dd36a08>
>>>
```

 NOTE   In this module, we will use the terms instance and object synonymously.

Lesson 7.2.1 Defining a Class in Python

In our example, we will be creating the blueprint for a person. Compared to most languages, the syntax for defining a simple class is very minimal in Python.

CREATING A CLASS

Next we will create our first class, called Person.

Declare the class using the Python keyword class, followed by the class name Person. In the block, we have the Python keyword pass, which is used as a placeholder for where the rest of our class definition will go as shown in **Snippet 7.3**.

Snippet 7.3

```
>>> class Person:
...     pass
...
>>>
```

If we run the `type` function on this class we have created; it will yield the type `type` as shown in **Snippet 7.4**.

Snippet 7.4

```
>>> type(Person)
<class 'type'>
>>>
```

This is a bit confusing, but what this means is just as there are data structures of type `list` or `dict`, we have also, in a sense, extended the Python language to include a new kind of data structure called `Person`. In Python, a `class` and a `type` are synonymous. This `Person` structure can encapsulate different attributes and methods that will be specific to that object. We will look at this in more depth further shortly.

Lesson 7.2.2 Instantiating an Object

Having a blueprint for building something is a great first step. However, blueprints aren't very useful if you can't build what they describe. Instantiating an object of a class is the act of building what the blueprint/class describes.

INSTANTIATING A PERSON OBJECT

From the `Person` class we have defined, we will instantiate a `Person` object.

Create a `Person` object and assign it to the `jack` variable as shown in **Snippet 7.5**.

Snippet 7.5

```
>>> jack = Person()
```

Create another object and assign it to the `jill` variable as shown in **Snippet 7.6**.

Snippet 7.6

```
>>> jill = Person()
```

Make a comparison between `jack` and `jill` to check whether they are different objects as shown in **Snippet 7.7**.

Snippet 7.7

```
>>> jack is jill
False
```

You will find that they are. This is because whenever we instantiate an object, it creates a brand-new object.

Assign `jack2` to `jack` as shown in **Snippet 7.8**.

Snippet 7.8

```
>>> jack2 = jack
>>> jack2 is jack
True
```

Assigning another variable to `jack` simply points it to whatever object `jack` is pointing to, and so they are the same object and thus identical.

Lesson 7.2.3 Adding Attributes to an Object

An attribute is a specific characteristic of an object.

In Python, you can add attributes dynamically to an already instantiated object by writing the name of the object followed by a dot (.) and the name of the attribute you want to add, and assigning it to a value as shown in **Snippet 7.9**.

Snippet 7.9

```
>>> person1 = Person()
>>> person1.name = "Gol D. Roger"
```

However, setting attributes in this manner is a bad practice, because it leads to hard-to-read code that is hard to debug. We will see the appropriate way of setting attributes later in this module.

You can get the value of an attribute by using a similar syntax as shown in **Snippet 7.10**.

Snippet 7.10

```
>>> person1.name
'Gol D. Roger'
>>>
```

Every object in Python comes with built-in attributes, such as __dict__, which is a dictionary that holds all of the attributes of the object. See the example in **Snippet 7.11**.

Snippet 7.11

```
>>> person1 = Person()
>>> person1.__dict__
{}
>>> person1.name = "Gol D. Roger"
>>> person1.age = 53
>>> person1.height_in_cm = 180
>>> person1.__dict__
{'age': 53, 'height_in_cm': 180, 'name': 'Gol D. Roger'}
>>> print(person1.name, person1.age, person1.height_in_cm)
Gol D. Roger 53 180
>>>
```

Lesson 7.2.4 The __init__ Method

The appropriate way to add attributes to an object is by defining them in the object's constructor method. A constructor method resides in the class and is called to create an object. It often takes arguments that are used in setting attributes of that instantiated object.

In Python, the constructor method for an object is named __init__. As its name suggests, it is called when initializing an object of a class. Because of this, you can use it to pass the initial attributes you want your object to be constructed with.

The hasattr() function checks whether an object has a specific attribute or method. When we call the hasattr() function on the Person class to check whether it has an __init__ method, it returns True as shown in **Snippet 7.12**. This applies for all instances of the class, too.

Snippet 7.12

```
>>> hasattr(Person, '__init__')
True
>>> person1 = Person()
>>> hasattr(person1, '__init__')
True
>>>
```

This method is here because it is inherited. We will be taking a closer look at what inheritance is later in this module.

We can define this constructor method in our class just like a function and specify attributes that will need to be passed in when instantiating an object, see **Snippet 7.13**.

Snippet 7.13

```
>>> class Person:
...     def __init__(self, name):
...         self.name = name
...
>>>
```

Earlier, we likened classes to blueprints for objects. In the preceding example, we are adding more details to that blueprint, and stating that every Person object that will be created should have a name attribute.

We have the arguments self and name in the __init__ method signature. The name argument refers to the person's name, while self refers to the object we're currently in the process of creating.

Remember, the __init__ method is called when instantiating objects of the Person class, and because every person has a different name, we need to be able to assign different values to different instances. Therefore, we attach our current object's name attribute in the line self.name = name.

Let's test this out.

Practice this concept by completing Practice Exercise 7.2: Adding Attributes to a Class.

Test yourself on this concept by completing Lab Activity 7.2: Defining a Class and Objects.

LESSON 7.3 METHODS IN A CLASS

In this lesson, we will look at class methods in detail.

Lesson 7.3.1 Defining Methods in a Class

So far, we have seen how to add attributes to an object. As we mentioned earlier, objects are also comprised of behaviors known as methods. Now we will take a look at how to add our own methods to classes.

CREATING A METHOD FOR OUR CLASS

We will rewrite our original `Person` class to include a `speak` method.

Create a `speak` method in our `Person` class, as shown in **Snippet 7.20**.

Snippet 7.20

```
>>> class Person:
...     def __init__(self, name, age, height_in_cm):
...         self.name = name
...         self.age = age
...         self.height_in_cm = height_in_cm
...     def speak(self):
...         print("Hello!")
...
>>>
```

The syntax for defining an instance method is familiar. We pass the argument `self` which, as in the `__init__` method, refers to the current object at hand. Passing `self` will allow us to get or set the object's attributes inside our function. It is always the first argument of an instance method.

You would instantiate an object and call the method we have defined using the code shown in **Snippet 7.21**.

Snippet 7.21

```
>>> adam = Person("Adam", 47, 193)
>>> adam.speak()
Hello!
>>>
```

We can also access instance attributes within instance methods. **Snippet 7.22** shows how we can modify our instance method to use instance attributes by using `self`.

Snippet 7.22

```
>>> class Person:
...     def __init__(self, name, age, height_in_cm):
...         self.name = name
...         self.age = age
...         self.height_in_cm = height_in_cm
...     def speak(self):
...         print(f"Hello! My name is {self.name}. I am {self.age}
years old.")
...
>>> adam = Person("Adam", 47, 193)
>>> lovelace = Person("Lovelace", 24, 178)
>>> lucre = Person("Lucre", 13, 154)
>>> adam.speak()
Hello! My name is Adam. I am 47 years old.
>>> lovelace.speak()
Hello! My name is Lovelace. I am 24 years old.
>>> lucre.speak()
Hello! My name is Lucre. I am 13 years old.
>>>
```

As you can see, the output is dependent on the object we are calling the method on. Please note that adding the f in the print statement before the opening quotation mark allows us to write a Python expression between curly braces that can refer to variables or literal values.

Lesson 7.3.2 Passing Arguments to Instance Methods

Just as with normal functions, you can pass arguments to methods in a class. Let's now learn how to pass arguments to instance methods.

We will improve on our Person class by creating a new method called greet that takes in an argument, person, which is a Person object.

Snippet 7.23 shows how we will define the greet method in the Person class.

Snippet 7.23

```
>>> class Person:
...     def __init__(self, name, age):
...         self.name = name
...         self.age = age
...     def speak(self):
...         print(f"Hello! My name is {self.name}. I am
{self.age} years old.")
...     def greet(self, person):
...         print(f"Hi {person.name}")
```

 NOTE   We do not have to specify the method return type as you would in statically typed languages such as Java.

Snippet 7.24 shows how we would instantiate two new `Person` objects and call the `greet` method.

Snippet 7.24

```
>>> joe = Person("Josef", 31)
>>> gabby = Person("Gabriela", 32)
>>> joe.greet(gabby)
Hi Gabriela
>>>
```

We can add condition statements to instance methods. **Snippet 7.25** shows how we would add more logic to the method that checks for the person's name, and prints out a different message if the person is named `Rogers`.

Snippet 7.25

```
>>> class Person:
...     def __init__(self, name, age):
...         self.name = name
...         self.age = age
...     def speak(self):
...         print(f"Hello! My name is {self.name}. I am
{self.age} years old.")
...     def greet(self, person):
...         if person.name == "Rogers":
...             print("Hey neighbor!")
...         else:
...             print(f"Hi {person.name}")
```

Snippet 7.26 shows how we could test out the new implementation of the `greet` method.

Snippet 7.26

```
>>> joe = Person("Josef", 31)
>>> john = Person("John", 5)
>>> rogers = Person("Rogers", 46)
>>> john.greet(rogers)
Hey neighbor!
>>> john.greet(joe)
Hi Josef
```

Lesson 7.3.3 Setting Instance Attributes within Instance Methods

You can also set instance attributes within instance methods. To expand on our example, we will create a `birthday` method that increments the person's age.

First we will implement the `birthday` method, which takes the age and increments it by 1 as shown in **Snippet 7.27**.

Snippet 7.27

```
>>> class Person:
...     def __init__(self, name, age):
...         self.name = name
...         self.age = age
...     def speak(self):
...         print(f"Hello! My name is {self.name}. I am
{self.age} years old.")
...     def birthday(self):
...         self.age += 1
```

Snippet 7.28 creates a person instance and checks the age.

Snippet 7.28

```
>>> diana = Person("Diana", 28)
>>> diana.age
28
```

Every time we call the birthday method, the age increases. **Snippet 7.29** calls the `birthday` method and checks the age again.

Snippet 7.29

```
>>> diana.birthday()
>>> diana.age
29
>>>
```

Congratulations, you can now define and use classes. You can add methods and attributes to them, as well as instantiate objects and use them. Although there is more to learn, you have the necessary tools to build basic object-oriented programs.

Test yourself on this concept by completing Lab Activity 7.3: Defining Methods in a Class.

LESSON 7.4 CLASS VERSUS INSTANCE ATTRIBUTES

In the previous lesson, we had an introduction to classes and attributes. The attributes we have seen defined up until this point are **instance attributes**. This means that they are bound to a specific instance. Initializing an object with specific attributes applies/binds those attributes to only that object, but not to any other object initialized from that class.

Practice this concept by completing Practice Exercise 7.4A: Declaring a Class with Instance Attributes.

Lesson 7.4.1 Class Attributes

We can also define attributes at the class level. **Class attributes** are bound to the class itself and are shared by all instances as opposed to being bound to each instance.

EXTENDING OUR CLASS WITH CLASS ATTRIBUTES

In this example, we will add a class attribute to our `WebBrowser` class from Practice Exercise 7.4A. The syntax for this is just like defining a variable. You simply define it in the class body.

We add the `connected` attribute to our class as shown in **Snippet 7.33**. This is a Boolean showing whether the web browser has an active Internet connection.

Snippet 7.33

```
class WebBrowser:
    connected = True
    def __init__(self, page):
        self.history = [page]
        self.current_page = page
        self.is_incognito = False
```

Snippet 7.34 instantiates `WebBrowser` objects. We can see that the `connected` attribute is `True` for both instances.

Snippet 7.34

```
>>> firefox = WebBrowser("google.com")
>>> iceweasel = WebBrowser("facebook.com")
>>> firefox.connected
True
>>> iceweasel.connected
True
>>>
```

Because a class attribute is bound to the class and not the instance, we can access class attributes via the class itself as shown in **Snippet 7.35**.

Snippet 7.35

```
>>> WebBrowser.connected
True
>>>
```

If we print out our instances' `__dict__` attributes; we will see that they do not have the `connected` attribute as shown in **Snippet 7.36**.

Snippet 7.36

```
>>> iceweasel.__dict__
{'history': ['facebook.com'], 'current_page': 'facebook.com',
'is_incognito': False}
>>> firefox.__dict__
{'history': ['google.com'], 'current_page': 'google.com',
'is_incognito': False}
>>>
```

Why, then, don't we get an `AttributeError` when we try to retrieve this attribute? This is because when we access a class attribute from an instance, it retrieves it from the class itself. In **Snippet 7.37** we can see that the `WebBrowser` class's `__dict__` contains the `connected` attribute.

Snippet 7.37

```
>>> WebBrowser.__dict__
mappingproxy({'__module__': '__main__', 'connected': True,
'__init__': <function WebBrowser.__init__ at 0x10cc6ad08>,
'__dict__': <attribute '__dict__' of 'WebBrowser' objects>,
'__weakref__': <attribute '__weakref__' of 'WebBrowser' objects>,
'__doc__': None})
>>>
```

> **NOTE** Because instances retrieve the attribute from the class, when we change this class attribute through the class, it will reflect on all existing instances.

Therefore, we need to be cautious when changing a class attribute through an instance, as shown in **Snippet 7.38**, because doing so will create an instance attribute and will no longer retrieve the attribute from the class.

Snippet 7.38

```
>>> firefox.connected = False
>>>
```

After changing the class attribute through the instance, we print out the `__dict__` attribute of the object and see that it now has a new instance attribute, `connected` as shown in **Snippet 7.39**.

Snippet 7.39

```
>>> firefox.__dict__
{'history': ['google.com'], 'current_page': 'google.com',
'is_incognito': False, 'connected': False}
>>>
```

This means that when we try to get the `connected` attribute, it will no longer try retrieving it from the class, but will instead retrieve the attribute bound to the object. Despite this change we have made, the `WebBrowser` class attribute remains the same as shown in **Snippet 7.40**.

Snippet 7.40

```
>>> WebBrowser.connected
True
>>>
```

Practice this concept by completing Practice Exercise 7.4B: Implementing a Counter for Instances of a Class.

NOTE Besides the use cases we've seen, class attributes should be used when you have variables that are common to all instances, such as constants for the class.

Test yourself on this concept by completing Lab Activity 7.4: Creating Class Attributes.

LESSON 7.5 CLASS VERSUS INSTANCE METHODS

In this lesson, we will take a brief look at instance methods and cover class methods in detail.

Lesson 7.5.1 Creating Instance Methods

Next, we will implement the `navigate` and `clear_history` methods for the `WebBrowser` class we defined in **Lesson 7.4**.

Snippet 7.47 shows the `navigate` method added to the `WebBrowser` class.

Snippet 7.47

```python
class WebBrowser:
    def __init__(self, page):
        self.history = [page]
        self.current_page = page
        self.is_incognito = False

    def navigate(self, new_page):
        self.current_page = new_page
        if not self.is_incognito:
            self.history.append(new_page)
```

Any call to `navigate` will the set the browser's current page to the `new_page` argument and then add it to the history if we are not in incognito mode (incognito mode in browsers prevents browsing history from being recorded).

Calling `navigate` on an instance should change `current_page` as shown in **Snippet 7.48**.

Snippet 7.48

```python
>>> vivaldi = WebBrowser("gocampaign.org")
>>> vivaldi.current_page
'gocampaign.org'
>>> vivaldi.navigate("reddit.com")
>>> vivaldi.current_page
'reddit.com'
>>> vivaldi.history
['gocampaign.org', 'reddit.com']
>>>
```

Create the `clear_history` method, which will delete the browser's history as shown in **Snippet 7.49**.

Snippet 7.49

```
class WebBrowser:
    def __init__(self, page):
        self.history = [page]
        self.current_page = page
        self.is_incognito = False

    def navigate(self, new_page):
        self.current_page = new_page
        if not self.is_incognito:
            self.history.append(new_page)

    def clear_history(self):
        self.history[:-1] = []
```

The `clear_history` method removes everything from the history list up to the last element, which is our current page. This leaves only our current page on the list.

In **Snippet 7.50** we add to the browser history by navigating to a couple of pages and then call the `clear_history` method to see whether it works.

Snippet 7.50

```
>>> chrome = WebBrowser("example.net")
>>> chrome.navigate("example2.net")
>>> chrome.navigate("example3.net")
>>> chrome.history
['example.net', 'example2.net', 'example3.net']
>>> chrome.current_page
'example3.net'
>>> chrome.clear_history()
>>> chrome.history
['example3.net']
>>>
```

We mentioned in Module 6: Dictionaries and Sets that instance methods must receive `self` as the first argument. This is because `self` refers to the current instance in the context. Despite not passing it as an argument when calling instance methods, our method calls execute without any error. How does this work?

Python passes the `self` argument implicitly. In **Snippet 7.50**, when we call `chrome.clear_history()`, Python essentially passes `chrome` in as an argument to the method; therefore, we don't need to explicitly pass in a value for `self`.

Such a method, one that takes an instance (`self`) as the first parameter, is referred to as a **bound method**. It is bound to that specific instance when it is created. In a sense, it can be thought of as every instance of a class having its own copy of the method that was defined in the class. If we print out the instance method of any instance, we will see output similar to that shown in **Snippet 7.51**.

Snippet 7.51

```
>>> chrome.navigate
<bound method WebBrowser.navigate of <__main__.WebBrowser object at
0x107a9a390>>
>>> opera = WebBrowser("foobar.com")
>>> opera.navigate
<bound method WebBrowser.navigate of <__main__.WebBrowser object at
0x107a9a400>>
>>>
```

The output for `chrome.navigate` tells us that it is a bound method of an object in the memory location `0x107a9a390`. The output of `opera.navigate` tells us that it is a bound method of a different object at memory location `0x107a9a400`. This shows us that the two instance methods are tied/bound to different objects.

Lesson 7.5.2 Class Methods

This brings us to class methods. **Class methods** differ from instance methods in that they are bound to the class itself and not the instance. As such, they don't have access to instance attributes. Additionally, they can be called through the class itself and don't require the creation of an instance of the class.

Regarding instance methods, we saw that the first parameter is always an instance; with class methods, the first parameter is always the class itself, as we will see in our examples.

One common use case for class methods is when you are making **factory methods**. A factory method is one that returns objects. They can be used for returning objects of a different type or with different attributes. Let's add a class method called `with_incognito` to our `WebBrowser` class that initializes a web browser object in incognito mode as shown in **Snippet 7.52**.

Snippet 7.52

```
class WebBrowser:
    def __init__(self, page):
        self.history = [page]
        self.current_page = page
        self.is_incognito = False

    def navigate(self, new_page):
        self.current_page = new_page
        if not self.is_incognito:
            self.history.append(new_page)

    def clear_history(self):
        self.history[:-1] = []

    @classmethod
    def with_incognito(cls, page):
        instance = cls(page)
        instance.is_incognito = True
        instance.history = []
        return instance
```

Our function definition begins with a peculiar piece of syntax, `@classmethod`. We won't go into the details on it; all we need to know right now is that it tells Python to add the function below it as a class method. On the next line, we declare our function, which takes two arguments, `cls` and `page`. The `cls` argument refers to our `WebBrowser` class in this context. All class methods must have the class as the first argument. The name can be `cls`, which is the convention, or anything else, whether it be `class_` or `foobar`. All that matters is that the first argument of the class method is *reserved*.

We pass the `page` argument during the instantiation of our `WebBrowser` object. In the function's body, we instantiate an object which we assign the name `instance`. We then change the incognito value of that instance to `True` and clear the history list. Finally, we return the instance we have created.

> Practice this concept by completing Practice Exercise 7.5A: Testing Our Factory Method.

 **CAUTION** You should only call class methods through an instance in situations where it won't raise any confusion as to what kind of method it is you are calling (instance or class method).

> Practice this concept by completing Practice Exercise 7.5B: Accessing Class Attributes from within Class Methods.

Lesson 7.5.3 Encapsulation and Information Hiding

One of the key concepts of OOP is **encapsulation**. Encapsulation is the bundling of data with the methods that operate on that data. It is used to hide the internal state of an object by bundling together and providing methods that can get and set the object state through an interface. This hiding of the internal state of an object is what we refer to as **information hiding**.

With our `WebBrowser` class, when we called the `navigate` method as users, all we cared about was that it changed the current page. The class was a bundle of data and logic that gave us access to a uniform browser interface. The same is true for a real web browser. As users, we simply type in the URL and hit the **Enter** key, and it takes us to the new page. We don't care to know that the browser had to make a request to the server, wait for the response, render the resulting markup, apply styling, and download accompanying media along with it. The browser acts as a simple interface that allows us to interact with the Internet. The processes behind all the steps it takes are hidden away from the users.

We use information hiding to abstract away irrelevant details about the class from users to prevent them from changing them, which would affect the functionality of our class.

In Python, information hiding is accomplished by marking attributes as `private` or `protected`:

- `private` attributes should only be used inside the class definition and shouldn't be accessed externally.
- `protected` attributes are similar to `private` ones, but can only be used in very specific contexts.

In most languages, these attribute access modifiers are denoted by the keyword `private`, `public`, or `protected`. Python, however, simply implements these in the attribute names themselves.

All Python attributes are `public` by default and need no special naming or declaration as shown in **Snippet 7.61**.

Snippet 7.61

```
class Car:
    def __init__(self):
        self.speed = 300
        self.color = "black"
```

For `protected` attributes, we prefix the attribute name with an underscore, _, to show that it is `protected` as shown in **Snippet 7.62**.

Snippet 7.62

```
class Car:
    def __init__(self):
        self.speed = 300
        self.color = "black"
```

Doing this doesn't change the class user's ability to change the attribute. It is simply a marker letting them know not to access or change the attribute from outside the class or its children. The interpreter enforces no actual restrictions to enforce this. You can still change `protected` attributes as shown in **Snippet 7.63**.

Snippet 7.63

```
>>> car = Car()
>>> car._speed
300
>>> car._speed = 400
>>> car._speed
400
>>>
```

Although it may seem that marking attribute names as `protected` is useless because it doesn't impose any restrictions, it is good practice to do it to let the users of the class know it is a `protected` attribute that is only meant to be used internally. It is up to them to follow convention and not assign or access `protected` attributes.

For `private` attributes, we prefix the attribute name with a double underscore __, as shown in **Snippet 7.64**. This renders the attribute inaccessible from outside the class. The attribute can only be gotten and set from within the class.

Snippet 7.64

```
class Car:
    def __init__(self):
        self.__speed = 300
        self.__color = "black"
    def change_speed(self, new_speed):
        self.__speed = new_speed
    def get_speed(self):
        return self.__speed
```

If we try accessing any of these attributes from outside the class, we will get an error as shown in **Snippet 7.65**.

Snippet 7.65

```
>>> car = Car()
>>> car.__speed
Traceback (most recent call last):
  File "<stdin>", line 1, in <module>
AttributeError: 'Car' object has no attribute '__speed'
>>>
```

To change the `private` attribute `__speed`, we need to use the defined setter method `change_speed`. Similarly, we can use the `get_speed` getter method to get the `speed` attribute from outside the class if need be as demonstrated in **Snippet 7.66**.

Snippet 7.66

```
>>> car.get_speed()
300
>>> car.change_speed(120)
>>> car.get_speed()
120
>>>
```

The table shown in **Figure 7.4** compares instance attributes with class attributes.

Instance attributes	Class attributes
Are bound to the instance	Are bound to the class
Can only be retrieved through the instance	Can be accessed through both the instance and class
Changing this value only changes it for the current instance	Changing this value changes it for all instances

Figure 7.4   Instance versus class attributes

The table shown in **Figure 7.5** compares instance methods with class methods.

Instance methods	Class methods
Are bound to the instance	Are bound to the class
Can only be called through an instance	Can be called through both the instance and the class
Take the self instance as the first argument	Take the class as the first argument
Have access to both instance and class attributes	Only have access to class attributes

Figure 7.5   Instance versus class methods

Test yourself on this concept by completing Lab Activity 7.5: Creating Class Methods and Using Information Hiding.

LESSON 7.6 CLASS INHERITANCE

A key feature of object-oriented programming is **inheritance**. Inheritance is a mechanism that allows for a class's implementation to be derived from another class's implementation. This subclass/derived/child class inherits all of the attributes and methods of the superclass/base/parent class as shown in **Figure 7.7**.

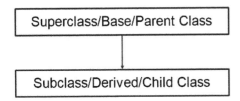

Figure 7.7   Inheritance in classes

A practical real-world example of inheritance can be thought of with big cats. Cheetahs, leopards, tigers, and lions are all cats. They all share the same properties that are common to cats such as mass, lifespan, speed, and behaviors such as making vocalizations and hunting, among others. If we were to implement a Leopard, Cheetah, or Lion class, we would define one Cat class that has all of these properties and then derive the Leopard, Lion, and Cheetah classes from this Cat class because they all share these same properties. This would be inheritance.

We use inheritance because it confers the following benefits:

- It makes our code more reusable. For example, with our Cat class example, we don't have to repeat the properties that each of the Lion, Cheetah, and Leopard classes possess; we can simply define them once in the Cat class and inherit the functionality in the derived classes. This also reduces code duplication.
- Inheritance also makes it easier to extend functionality because a method or attribute added to a base class automatically gets applied to all of its subclasses. For example, defining a spots attribute in the Cat class automatically avails cheetah and leopard subclasses with the same attribute.
- Inheritance adds flexibility to our code. Any place where a superclass instance is being used, a subclass instance can be substituted for the same effect. For example, at any place where a Cat instance would be used in our code, a Leopard, Lion, or Cheetah instance can be substituted because they are all cats.

The Python syntax for inheritance is very minimal. You define the class as usual, but then you can pass in the base class as a parameter as shown in **Snippet 7.68**. As we will see in **Lesson 7.7**, you can pass multiple base classes for cases in which you want multiple inheritance.

Snippet 7.68

```
class Subclass(Superclass):
    pass
```

Something that goes hand-in-hand with inheritance is the concept of overriding. Let's assume our Cat class has a vocalize method that prints the default sound a cat makes. Leopards and lions may make a different sound from the one defined in the Cat class's vocalize method. In a case like this, you would override the vocalize method in the subclass. **Overriding** means redefining the implementation of a method defined in a superclass to add or change a subclass's functionality.

We' will be taking a look at overriding in more depth in the next lesson.

Practice this concept by completing Practice Exercise 7.6: Implementing Class Inheritance.

Lesson 7.6.1 Overriding_init_()

In Practice Exercise 7.6 we overrode the `vocalize` method of our `Cat` base class in our `Cheetah`, `Lion`, and `Leopard` subclasses. In this lesson, we will see how to override the __init__ method.

A lot of big cats have a pattern in their coat; they have spots or stripes. Let's add this to our `Cheetah` subclass.

OVERRIDING THE __INIT__ METHOD TO ADD AN ATTRIBUTE

Let's override the initializer method and add the `spotted_coat` attribute to the `Cheetah` class as shown in **Snippet 7.76**.

Snippet 7.76

```python
class Cat:
    def __init__(self, mass, lifespan, speed):
        self.mass_in_kg = mass
        self.lifespan_in_years = lifespan
        self.speed_in_kph = speed

    def vocalize(self):
        print("Chuff")

    def print_facts(self):
        print(f"The {type(self).__name__.lower()} "
            f"weighs {self.mass_in_kg}kg,"
            f" has a lifespan of {self.lifespan_in_years} years and
"
            f"can run at a maximum speed of
{self.speed_in_kph}kph.")

class Cheetah(Cat):
    def __init__(self, mass, lifespan, speed):
        self.spotted_coat = True

    def vocalize(self):
        print("Chirrup")
```

Unfortunately, this overwrites the previous implementation of __init__ and replaces it with our new one; so, when we initialize the `Cheetah` subclass, it won't add the `mass_in_kg`, `lifespan_in_years`, and `speed_in_kph` attributes. It will only add the `spotted_coat` attribute to the instance.

Snippet 7.77 initializes the newly modified `Cheetah` class. It raises an error upon trying to access the original attributes that it had before we overrode the __init__ method.

Snippet 7.77

```
>>> cheetah = Cheetah(72, 12, 120)
>>> cheetah.mass_in_kg
Traceback (most recent call last):
  File "<stdin>", line 1, in <module>
AttributeError: 'Cheetah' object has no attribute 'mass_in_kg'
>>> cheetah.lifespan_in_years
Traceback (most recent call last):
  File "<stdin>", line 1, in <module>
AttributeError: 'Cheetah' object has no attribute 'lifespan_in_years'
>>> cheetah.speed_in_kph
Traceback (most recent call last):
  File "<stdin>", line 1, in <module>
AttributeError: 'Cheetah' object has no attribute 'speed_in_kph'
>>> cheetah.spotted_coat
True
>>>
```

What we can do is invoke the __init__ method of the Cat class inside the Cheetah subclass's __init__ method before adding the spotted_coat attribute. To do this, we can call Cat.__init__(self, mass, lifespan, speed), which calls the superclass's initializer with the required arguments, as shown in **Snippet 7.78**.

Snippet 7.78

```
class Cheetah(Cat):
    def __init__(self, mass, lifespan, speed):
        Cat.__init__(self, mass, lifespan, speed)
        self.spotted_coat = True

    def vocalize(self):
        print("Chirrup")
```

However, doing this hardcodes the superclass name, and in case we need to change the name of the Cat class, we'd have to change it in multiple places. Python provides a cleaner way of doing this through the built-in super method. We use super to access inherited methods from a parent class that has been overwritten in the child class, as shown in **Snippet 7.79**.

Snippet 7.79

```
class Cheetah(Cat):
    def __init__(self, mass, lifespan, speed):
        super().__init__(mass, lifespan, speed)
        self.spotted_coat = True

    def vocalize(self):
        print("Chirrup")
```

When we instantiate a `Cheetah` instance, we see that our `Cat` superclass implementation is preserved, as shown in **Snippet 7.80**.

Snippet 7.80

```
>>> cheetah = Cheetah(72,12,120)
>>> cheetah.print_facts()
The cheetah weighs 72kg, has a lifespan of 12 years and can run at a
maximum speed of 120kph.
>>>
```

At the same time, our new implementation is also added as seen in **Snippet 7.81**.

Snippet 7.81

```
>>> cheetah.spotted_coat
True
>>>
```

Lesson 7.6.2 Commonly Overridden Methods

As you may have noticed, special methods in Python classes are always prefixed and suffixed with double underscores, for example, __init__. They are known as **Dunder (double underscore)** or **magic methods**.

Besides the __init__ method, there are other magic methods in Python that you can override to customize your class and add custom functionality, such as changing what the output of your printed object looks like or how your classes are compared.

We will only be going over the method that defines what is output when print is called on your object, __str__, and the method that is called when an object is destroyed, __del__.

Lesson 7.6.3 The __str__() Method

Every object in Python has the __str__ method by default. It is called every time print is called on an object in Python to retrieve the string containing the readable representation of the object.

Let's replace the print_facts method of the Cat class with this method as shown in **Snippet 7.82**.

Snippet 7.82

```
class Cat:
    def __init__(self, mass, lifespan, speed):
        self.mass_in_kg = mass
        self.lifespan_in_years = lifespan
        self.speed_in_kph = speed

    def vocalize(self):
        print("Chuff")

    def __str__(self):
        return f"The {type(self).__name__.lower()} "\
                f"weighs {self.mass_in_kg}kg,"\
                f" has a lifespan of {self.lifespan_in_years} years and "\
                f"can run at a maximum speed of {self.speed_in_kph}kph."
```

Now, when we call `print` on any `Cat` instance or `Cat` subclass instance, it should have the same result as when we were calling `print_facts` as seen in **Snippet 7.83**.

Snippet 7.83

```
>>> cheetah = Cheetah(72, 12, 120)
>>> print(cheetah)
The cheetah weighs 72kg, has a lifespan of 12 years and can run at a
maximum speed of 120kph.
>>>
```

Lesson 7.6.4 The __del__() Method

The `__del__` method is the destructor method. The destructor method is called whenever an object gets destroyed. Let's override this method as shown in **Snippet 7.84**.

Snippet 7.84

```
class Cheetah(Cat):
    def __init__(self, mass, lifespan, speed):
        super().__init__(mass, lifespan, speed)
        self.spotted_coat = True

    def vocalize(self):
        print("Chirrup")

    def __del__(self):
        print("No animals were harmed in the deletion of this instance")
```

If we call `del` on a `Cheetah` instance, it should print out that message as shown in **Snippet 7.85**.

Snippet 7.85

```
>>> cheetah = Cheetah(72, 12, 120)
>>> del cheetah
No animals were harmed in the deletion of this instance
>>> cheetah
Traceback (most recent call last):
  File "<stdin>", line 1, in <module>
NameError: name 'cheetah' is not defined
>>>
```

Test yourself on this concept by completing Lab Activity 7.6: Overriding Methods.

LESSON 7.7 MULTIPLE INHERITANCE

Multiple inheritance is a feature that allows you to inherit attributes and methods from more than one class. The most common use case for multiple inheritance is for **mixins**. Mixins are classes that have methods/attributes that are meant to be used by other functions. For example, a `Logger` class would have a `log` method that writes to a logfile, and when added to your classes as a mixin, would give them that same capability.

Snippet 7.87 shows the syntax for multiple inheritance.

Snippet 7.87

```
class Subclass(Superclass1, Superclass2):
  pass
```

The subclass inherits all of the features of both superclasses.

Practice this concept by completing Practice Exercise 7.7: Implementing Multiple Inheritance.

Test yourself on this concept by completing Lab Activity 7.7: Practicing Multiple Inheritance.

SUMMARY

In this module, we have begun our journey into OOP. OOP makes code more reusable; it makes it easier to design software; it makes code easier to test, debug, and maintain; and it adds a form of security to the data in an application.

The behaviors of an object are known as methods, and you can add a method to a class by defining a function inside it. To be bound to your objects, this function needs to take in the argument `self`. We also covered class attributes and class methods in detail.

We also took a look at encapsulation and the keywords that enable information hiding in Python. Information hiding is used to abstract away irrelevant details about the class from users.

This module also covered inheritance in detail. We saw how to have a derived class inherit from a single base class, as well as multiple base classes. We also saw how to override methods: specifically, the __init__, __str__, and __del__ methods. This module completes our journey into object-oriented programming with Python.

In the next module, **Module 8: Modules, Packages, and File Operations**, we will cover Python modules and packages in detail. We will also take a look at how to handle different types of files and related file operations.

MODULES, PACKAGES, AND FILE OPERATIONS

MODULE OBJECTIVES

BY THE END OF THIS MODULE, YOU WILL BE ABLE TO:

1. Describe what Python modules are and create your own
2. Describe what Python packages are and create your own
3. Work with the built-in Python modules
4. Describe the `file` object in Python
5. Read and write to Python files
6. Work with structured data in Python files

INTRODUCTION

This module introduces Python modules and packages. We also cover file operations available to us in Python.

In the previous module, **Module 7: Object-Oriented Programming**, we covered object-oriented programming in depth. We covered important OOP concepts such as classes, methods, and inheritance. In this module, we will take a look at modules and file operations.

When you are working on any project, for example, a Word document, you may have a folder with the name of your project, and inside it you have the project files themselves. This helps you know which files are associated with which project. Next time you want to look at the project files, you won't have to search all over your computer for them. You can simply go to the project folder and find the files you need.

The concept of arranging work into files and folders also applies when programming in Python. You can arrange your code into pieces called **modules**, which makes it easier to group related functionality together. After you have created a module, it becomes very easy to refer to that collection of functionalities again and also share and reuse the functionality defined in that module.

Specifically, a module in Python is any file with a `.py` extension. A Python module can contain any valid Python code you want, including classes, functions, or just variable definitions. After you have created a module, you can then import it elsewhere to use whatever resources are defined in the module.

A module can also be a directory containing Python files. Adding an `__init__.py` file inside a directory will tell the Python interpreter that the indicated directory is a module and that it will be registered in Python's module namespace. Note that it is no longer a requirement to have an `__init__.py` file, but it is a good practice to have one in case you need to run some custom code during module initialization.

Following the same trend, a **package** is, therefore, defined as a collection of modules. Packages are a good way of separating your modules from other people's modules to avoid name clashes.

Arranging your code into modules and packages makes it extremely easy for other developers to work with your code. They can easily see what resources are defined in each package or module and import them as needed.

Real-life applications will need to read input from files or write output to files at one point or another. Every time you open a document, be it a PDF file, a JPEG image, or even a `.py` file in your application, some code is running behind the scenes to process that file and output the data to you.

Imagine a payroll system. The system may be implemented in a way where user data is input into an Excel sheet containing the name of the person and the hours worked in a specific time period. The program will then read this data and calculate the amount of wages each person is owed and output a new file with the name of the person and their wages.

Does this sound interesting? This is just an example of what you can do after you can read input from a file. Files are useful for aggregating huge amounts of data that might be too cumbersome to enter through the keyboard line by line.

Imagine if the aforementioned payroll system needed input to be entered on the keyboard by hand. This would make payroll processing, for whatever company that used it, very cumbersome and prone to mistakes.

On the other hand, a file could contain thousands of lines, and the execution of the payroll would be faster because the input is not blocked by data entry. In fact, we shall build a rudimentary version of such a payroll system at the end of this module after you have a deeper understanding of how to work with files in Python.

LESSON 8.1 DEFINING MODULES

Following the definition of a module that was given earlier, you can now see that you have, in fact, been working with modules all along. Any valid `.py` file that you have created in this course is more or less a valid module.

In this lesson, though, we are going to be a bit more deliberate in how we create modules so that you can see how to define and import resources.

To recap, a valid Python module is any `.py` file containing valid Python code. This code could be variable definitions, functions, classes, methods, and so on. We are going to practice with a simple module that contains just one function.

Let's go ahead and create our first module.

Lesson 8.1.1 Creating Modules

Let's create a module named `calculator`.

First we will create a file named `calculator.py`. This is where our module resources are going to be stored.

Inside the file, we will add the simple function code shown in **Snippet 8.1** in order to add and return the sum of two numbers.

Snippet 8.1

```
def add(x, y):
    return x + y
```

Remember, the def keyword is used to define functions in Python. In our example, we are defining a function called add that takes two parameters, x and y, which will both be integers. The function body simply returns the sum of the two numbers by using the + operator.

Next, let's run the Python interpreter using the Python command in the same folder you created the calculator module in.

You can now see and use the function you defined by importing the calculator module as shown in **Snippet 8.2**.

Snippet 8.2

```
>>> import calculator
>>> calculator.add(8, 9)
17
```

Module names should follow normal Python variable naming conventions. These include the following:

- They should follow snake_case (lower_case_with_underscore). Some good module names would be module and another_module. The following are examples of bad module names: Amodule and AnotherModule.
- Names should be descriptive. This means that the module name should reflect the purpose of the resources defined inside it; for example, a module containing mathematical functions should be named math, but not string.
- Only use underscores if it improves readability.

When importing a module, the code in the module is executed exactly once, even if you have another statement in the code importing the exact same module elsewhere. Upon import, Python compiles the module's code, executes the code, and then populates the module's namespace with the resource names defined in the module. This makes the resources that have been imported accessible in the scope in which they have been imported.

Some best practices include using four spaces for indentation, using snake_case for variable names, and so on. The following are some examples:

1. Naming variables, functions, modules – lowercase_with_underscores.
2. Naming classes – CapitalizeFirstLetters.
3. Avoid variable names like k, c, and so on, except where their meanings can be derived from the context, for example, looping.
4. Use comments sparingly.
5. Write tests.

Practice this concept by completing Practice Exercise 8.1: Creating and Importing a User-Defined Module.

LESSON 8.2 IMPORTS AND IMPORT STATEMENTS

There are several ways we can import and use the resources defined in a module. Taking the `calculator` module we defined previously, you have already seen one way to go about it, which is importing the whole module by using the `import` keyword and then calling a resource inside it by using the dot (.) notation, as shown in **Snippet 8.8**.

Snippet 8.8

```
>>> import calculator
>>> calculator.add(8, 9)
17
```

Another way of accessing a module's resources is to use the `from...import...` syntax shown in **Snippet 8.9**.

Snippet 8.9

```
>>> from calculator import *
>>> add(8, 9)
17
```

Note that the * in the preceding example tells Python to import everything in the module named `calculator`. We can then use any resource defined in the `calculator` module by referring to the resource name (in our case, the `add` function) directly. You should note that using * is not a good practice. You should always strive to import exactly what you need.

What if you want to only import a few resources from the module? In that case, you can name them directly, as shown in **Snippet 8.10**.

Snippet 8.10

```
>>> from calculator import add
>>> add(8, 9)
17
```

Another useful thing you can do is name your imports by using the `as` keyword, as shown in **Snippet 8.11**.

Snippet 8.11

```
>>> from calculator import add as a
>>> a(8, 9)
17
>>> import calculator as calc
>>> calc.add(8, 9)
17
```

This can come in handy when you have a module or resource with a long name that you will be referring to in many places.

You can also group many imports by using parentheses for easier readability as shown in **Snippet 8.12**.

Snippet 8.12

```
>>> from random import (choice, choices)
```

Practice this concept by completing Practice Exercise 8.2A: Importing Modules.

Practice this concept by completing Practice Exercise 8.2B: Importing Functions from User-Defined Modules.

LESSON 8.3 MODULES AND PACKAGES

In this lesson, we will turn our focus toward the standard Python modules and Python packages.

Lesson 8.3.1 The Module Search Path

When you import any module, Python will first check whether there is a built-in module with the specified name. An example of a built-in module is the string module.

If no built-in module is found, the interpreter will look for a file with the name of the module and the .py extension in the directories given by the sys.path variable. This variable is simply a list of strings which specifies where to search for modules.

How this variable is built is beyond the scope of this course. However, it is partly dependent on your defined PYTHONPATH and can be modified if necessary. You can read more about it in the Python documentation at https://docs.python.org/3/library/sys.html#sys.path.

For your interest, though, you can inspect the sys.path in your current environment by running the commands shown in **Snippet 8.18**. Please note that your results will differ.

Snippet 8.18

```
>>> import sys
>>> sys.path
['', '/usr/local/bin',
'/usr/local/Cellar/python3/3.6.4_2/Frameworks/Python.framework/Versions/3.6
/lib/python36.zip',
'/usr/local/Cellar/python3/3.6.4_2/Frameworks/Python.framework/Versions/3.6
/lib/python3.6',
'/usr/local/Cellar/python3/3.6.4_2/Frameworks/Python.framework/Versions/3.6
/lib/python3.6/lib-dynload',
'/usr/local/Cellar/python3/3.6.4_2/Frameworks/Python.framework/Versions/3.6
/lib/python3.6/site- packages']
>>>
```

Lesson 8.3.2 Standard Python Modules

Python ships with many ready-made modules and packages. These modules and packages are grouped into libraries and are provided for use in the standard library.

An example is the `math` module, which provides utility functions for math operations.

Figure 8.1 shows several common modules that you are likely to interact with and what they do.

Module Name	Function
string	Has functions for working with and generating strings
math	Has mathematical functions such as `ceil()`, `floor()`, and `factorial()`
unittest	Contains assertions to help in writing unit tests for your code
sys	Help access system-specific functionality
os	Helps in using OS-specific functionality in a platform-agnostic way
urlib	A collection of modules for working with URLs, for example, sending HTTP requests and parsing URLS
datetime	A module for working with dates, time and timezones
random	A module for generating pseudo-random numbers following a specific spec
re	A module for working with regular expressions
itertools	A very useful library with optimized tools for more efficient iteration over collections such as lists
functools	Provides functions that operate on and return on other functions (commonly knows as higher-order functions). A common use case is for writing decorators.

Figure 8.1 **Common Python modules**

You can import each module and use the `dir()` function to see a list of the methods implemented in each. **Snippet 8.19** uses the `sys` module as an example.

Snippet 8.19

```
>>> import sys
>>> dir(sys)
['__displayhook__', '__doc__', '__excepthook__', '__interactivehook__',
'__loader__', '__name__', '__package__', '__spec__', '__stderr__',
'__stdin__', '__stdout__', '_clear_type_cache', '_current_frames',
'_debugmallocstats', '_getframe', '_git', '_home', '_xoptions', 'abiflags',
'api_version', 'argv', 'base_exec_prefix', 'base_prefix',
'builtin_module_names', 'byteorder', 'call_tracing', 'callstats',
'copyright', 'displayhook', 'dont_write_bytecode', 'exc_info',
'excepthook', 'exec_prefix', 'executable', 'exit', 'flags', 'float_info',
'float_repr_style', 'get_asyncgen_hooks', 'get_coroutine_wrapper',
'getallocatedblocks', 'getcheckinterval', 'getdefaultencoding',
'getdlopenflags', 'getfilesystemencodeerrors', 'getfilesystemencoding',
'getprofile', 'getrecursionlimit', 'getrefcount', 'getsizeof',
'getswitchinterval', 'gettrace', 'hash_info', 'hexversion',
'implementation', 'int_info', 'intern', 'is_finalizing', 'last_traceback',
'last_type', 'last_value', 'maxsize', 'maxunicode', 'meta_path', 'modules',
'path', 'path_hooks', 'path_importer_cache', 'platform', 'prefix',
'set_asyncgen_hooks', 'set_coroutine_wrapper', 'setcheckinterval',
'setdlopenflags', 'setprofile', 'setrecursionlimit', 'setswitchinterval',
'settrace', 'stderr', 'stdin', 'stdout', 'thread_info', 'version',
'version_ info', 'warnoptions']
>>>
```

You can also use the `help()` function in the same way as `dir()` to find more information about what a specific module does. The `help` function shows the content of **documentation strings (docstrings)** defined on the resource.

For example, we can add a docstring to our previous `calculator` function so that future users can find out what the function does as shown in **Snippet 8.20**.

Snippet 8.20

```
def add(x, y):
    """Return the sum of x and y."""
    return x + y
```

You can then use `help()` on it as shown in **Snippet 8.21**.

Snippet 8.21

```
>>> help(add)
```

The output will be similar to **Snippet 8.22**.

Snippet 8.22

```
Help on function add in module calculator:

add(x, y)
   Return the sum of x and y.
```

This is a best practice, and you should always strive to ensure that all your resources have docstring comments.

Practice this concept by completing Practice Exercise 8.3: Inspecting Modules and Packages.

Test yourself on this concept by completing Lab Activity 8.3A: Inspecting Modules.

Lesson 8.3.3 Packages

Packages are collections of modules. Each package must contain an __init__.py in the root of its directory, which indicates to the Python interpreter that the directory is a package.

The file doesn't need to contain anything, but you can use it for some added functionality (for example, to specify exactly what can and cannot be imported from the package).

When importing a package, the code in the __init__.py file is executed by the Python interpreter to build the package and the package namespace.

A sample package could have a file structure such as that shown in **Snippet 8.33**.

Snippet 8.33

```
mytools
|
├── __init__.py
├── calculator.py
├── tokenizer.py
```

In our example, the `mytools` package has two modules, the `calculator` and `tokenizer` modules. Sample imports would look like **Snippet 8.34**.

Snippet 8.34

```
# import both modules
from mytools import calculator, tokenizer

# import one of the modules
from mytools import calculator

# import specific resources from a module
from mytools.calculator import add, another_function
```

Lesson 8.3.4 Absolute Imports

An **absolute import** is an import that uses the full path from a project to the module being imported. An example of this is importing a built-in library as shown in **Snippet 8.35**.

Snippet 8.35

```
import string
```

Lesson 8.3.5 Relative Imports

A **relative import** is one that uses the relative path from the current directory to the directory where a module is located. Imports similar to the one shown in **Snippet 8.36** are relative.

Snippet 8.36

```
from . import calculator
```

The statement in Snippet 8.36 imports `calculator` from the current directory, which is represented by the dot (.).

 NOTE   Always prefer absolute imports where possible.

Test yourself on this concept by completing Lab Activity 8.3B: Listing the Resources Defined in a Package or Module.

Test yourself on this concept by completing Lab Activity 8.3C: Using Resources in a Module.

LESSON 8.4 FILE OPERATIONS

Files could be of many types, for example, text files with `.txt` extensions, data files in a `.csv` extension, or even executable files with `.exe` extensions. Not all file types are immediately readable. Some file types are proprietary and require specialized software to read them. An example of a proprietary file type is the PSD file that's generated by Adobe Photoshop.

We will be working with non-proprietary extensions which are easy to work with, such as `.txt`, `.csv`, and `.json` files for the purposes of this module. The skills that you will learn about will be transferrable to any other file you need to read with Python in the future.

LESSON 8.5 THE FILE OBJECT

The `file` object is the default and easiest way to manipulate files in Python. It includes a couple of methods and attributes which make it easier for developers to read from, and write to, files in the filesystem.

There are two major `file` object types that are recognized in Python:

- Binary `file` objects: These can read and write byte-like objects.
- Text `file` objects: These can read and write string objects.

The `open` function, which we will be looking at in **Lesson 8.6**, is the easiest way to create a `file` object. Depending on the mode passed to the `open` function, you will get back either a binary or text file object. We will be specifically working with text `file` objects.

Lesson 8.5.1 The File Object Methods

The `file` object has several methods to make it easy to work with the underlying file. They include the following:

- `file.read()`: This method loads the entire file into memory.
- `file.readline()`: This method reads a single line from the file into memory.
- `file.readlines()`: This method reads all of the lines of a file into a list.
- `file.write()`: This method writes output to the file.
- `file.seek()`: This method is used to move the `file` object position to a certain location in the file.

LESSON 8.6 READING AND WRITING TO FILES

In **Lesson 8.5**, we mentioned that to create a `file` object, you can use the built-in `open` function with a filename and mode parameter. But how exactly does that work? Let's talk a bit more about the open method now.

Lesson 8.6.1 The open() Function

The open function is a built-in function in Python that you can use to read a file. It takes two arguments, the filename and a mode, for example, open(name_of_file, mode), and returns a file object that you can manipulate.

The mode passed to the function determines what kind of file object you will get back and what you will be able to do with it. Some available modes are listed in **Figure 8.2**.

Mode	Use
r	Read mode. Only allows reading.
w	Write mode. Used to write data to a file. Overwrites any existing files with the same name.
a	Append mode. This is the same as the write mode, except it adds the data to the end of the file if it exists (or creates a new file if not).
r+	Handles both reading and writing

Figure 8.2   Available modes with open()

The table in Figure 8.2 lists the most important modes you will encounter. Some additional specialized modes are shown in **Figure 8.3**.

Mode	Use
rb	Reads a binary file
wb	Writes to a binary file
rb+	Combined special mode for working with binary file objects

Figure 8.3   Specialized modes with open()

Lesson 8.6.2 Creating, Reading, and Writing to Files

Let's learn how to create, read, and write to files.

First, we will focus on creating a file. To create a file in the Python interpreter, we can use the open function in, as shown in **Snippet 8.40**.

Snippet 8.40

```
>>> f = open('myfile.txt', 'w')
```

You should not see any output after running the command in Snippet 8.40. What it does is simple; we open a file called myfile.txt in the write mode. Because that file does not exist, a blank file with that name will be created on your filesystem. The file object that's created is assigned to the variable f, which you can then use to manipulate the file.

We can practice writing to the file as shown in **Snippet 8.41**.

Snippet 8.41

```
>>> f.write("Hello, world\n")
13
```

We used the `write` method on the `file` object to write the string `"Hello, world"` and a new line character to the file. You can see that `13` is the output. The `write` method returns the number of characters written.

We can write something else, as shown in **Snippet 8.42**.

Snippet 8.42

```
>>> f.write("Hello, world again")
18
```

Now close the file using the `close` method as shown in **Snippet 8.43**. This will write the contents to the file. Remember to always do this after you have finished working with a file:

Snippet 8.43

```
f.close()
```

If you check the contents of `myfile.txt` you should see the two strings we wrote, as shown in **Snippet 8.44**.

Snippet 8.44

```
Hello, world
Hello, world again
```

If we wanted to add more content to the file, we would open it in append mode as shown in **Snippet 8.45**. Note that if we opened the file again in w mode, it would erase all existing contents.

Snippet 8.45

```
>>> f = open('myfile.txt', 'a')
>>> f.write("More content")
12
>>> f.close()
```

`myfile.txt` should have the content shown in **Snippet 8.46**.

Snippet 8.46

```
Hello, world
Hello, world againMore content
```

The last two lines are joined because we did not write any new line character between them to the file.

To read the file, use the r mode of the `open` function, as shown in **Snippet 8.47**.

Snippet 8.47

```
>>> f = open('myfile.txt', 'r')
>>> f.read()
'Hello, world\nHello, world againMore content'
```

You cannot write in this mode, as shown in **Snippet 8.48**.

Snippet 8.48

```
>>> f.write("Some content")
Traceback (most recent call last):
  File "<input>", line 1, in <module>
    f.write("Some content")
io.UnsupportedOperation: not writable
>>> f.close()
```

Similarly, you cannot **read** in write (w) or append (a) modes as seen in **Snippet 8.49**.

Snippet 8.49

```
>>> f = open('myfile.txt', 'a')
>>> f.read()
Traceback (most recent call last):
  File "<input>", line 1, in <module>
    f.read()
io.UnsupportedOperation: not readable
>>> f.close()
>>> f = open('myfile.txt', 'w')
>>> f.read()
Traceback (most recent call last):
  File "<input>", line 1, in <module>
    f.read()
io.UnsupportedOperation: not readable
>>> f.close()
```

If you need to combine both reading and writing, use the r+ mode as shown in **Snippet 8.50**.

Snippet 8.50

```
>>> f = open('myfile.txt', 'r+')
>>> f.read()
''
>>> f.write("Some content")
13
```

Note that the r+ mode appends to the existing file when writing, so it is safe to use on existing files.

Practice this concept by completing Practice Exercise 8.6A: Creating and Writing to a Text File.

Lesson 8.6.3 The with Context Manager

Now that you understand the different file reading and writing modes, let's talk about automating some of the processes around working with files—more specifically, autoclosing files after you have finished using them. Remember, we need to close files after using them so that they can be removed from memory and so the memory is then freed up for other processes.

Python comes with a handy context manager for working with files, which helps in writing neater code and freeing resources automatically when the code exits so that you do not have to remember to do it. The syntax is shown in **Snippet 8.55**.

Snippet 8.55

```
with open("myfile.txt", "r+") as f:
    content = f.read()

    print(content)
```

This code will read the specified file for us, print the content, and exit while automatically closing the file.

You can also process each line individually (this can be done with or without the context manager, so long as you have a file object) as shown in **Snippet 8.56**.

Snippet 8.56

```
with open("myfile.txt") as f:
    for line in f:
        print(line)
```

Practice this concept by completing Practice Exercise 8.6B: Read Using with Keyword.

Test yourself on this concept by completing Lab Activity 8.6: Performing File Operations.

LESSON 8.7 HANDLING STRUCTURED DATA

Now that you have a good handle on reading and writing to files, let's talk about how to deal with more structured data. In real-world applications, you will most likely have to read data in a structured format.

Do you remember the payroll application we talked about in the beginning of this module? Such data could be represented in a **CSV file**. A CSV file is a file with **comma-separated values**, usually arranged in columns.

Such data can then be easily read into a spreadsheet application, such as Excel, and manipulated there. Python provides a utility to work with CSV files, which we will cover in this lesson.

Snippet 8.68 shows an example of a CSV file.

Snippet 8.68

```
Name,City
"Nash, Colorado B.",Milton Keynes
"Herrera, Chase E.",Gentbrugge
"Hubbard, Leilani I.",Bremen
"Vinson, Marsden H.",Lakeland County
"Macias, Lawrence E.",Noisy-le-Grand
...

...
"Phelps, Amity V.",Morena
"Woods, Jaden V.",Portland
"Hyde, Duncan P.",Schellebelle
"Hendricks, Yoshio V.",Sperlinga
"Delgado, Emma T.",Reyhanlı
"Oneil, Orson B.",Rotello
"Sims, Noah C.",Selkirk
```

CSV files are popular because they have some advantages over files such as spreadsheets; for example:

- They are human readable and easy to parse.
- They are smaller, compact, and faster to work with.
- CSV files are easy to generate and have a standard format.

Another form of structured data is **JSON**. JSON is very useful, especially on the Internet, for easily transferring data in the form of key-value pairs. JSON data looks like the sample given in **Snippet 8.69**.

Snippet 8.69

```
{
  "data": [
    {
      "name": "Rodriguez, Evangeline U.",
      "city": "Lobbes"
    },
    {
      "name": "Herman, Leandra P.",
      "city": "Tramonti di Sopra"
    }
  ]
}
```

Other formats used to transfer data over the Internet include:

- XML (you can learn more about XML at https://www.w3schools.com/xml/)
- Protocol buffers (you can learn more about protocol buffers at https://developers . google.com/protocol-buffers/)

Lesson 8.7.1 Working with CSV Data

Python includes the very handy `csv` module to help us work with CSV files. It makes it very easy to read the tabular data defined in a CSV file and operate on it by creating reader or writer objects.

For the following practice exercise, we will be using a CSV file of mock data, generated at random from the website Mockaroo. The file is called MOCK_DATA.csv. The raw data is as shown in **Figure 8.4**.

```
MOCK_DATA.csv - Notepad
File  Edit  Format  View  Help
id,first_name,last_name,email,gender,ip_address
1,Floris,Reuven,freuven0@zdnet.com,Female,217.240.50.206
2,Randall,Kulvear,rkulvear1@cbslocal.com,Male,34.22.91.187
3,Catha,Ladell,cladell2@soup.io,Female,189.132.194.151
4,Orson,Vicarey,ovicarey3@mashable.com,Male,101.17.139.15
5,Analise,Symms,asymms4@gov.uk,Female,189.62.145.112
6,Tucky,Corinton,tcorinton5@state.tx.us,Male,6.11.177.218
7,Edie,Wilsdon,ewilsdon6@senate.gov,Female,0.165.34.111
8,Frasquito,Petrelli,fpetrelli7@slate.com,Male,26.249.196.182
9,Rea,Ferneyhough,rferneyhough8@hubpages.com,Female,20.79.200.107
10,Latia,Borton,lborton9@bbc.co.uk,Female,114.152.84.232
11,Livvyy,Seczyk,lseczyka@mozilla.com,Female,30.26.231.161
12,Nolan,Everwin,neverwinb@loc.gov,Male,180.39.202.1
13,Devlin,Canaan,dcanaanc@friendfeed.com,Male,173.216.232.38
14,Madella,Crews,mcrewsd@netlog.com,Female,200.110.39.42
15,Noelani,Toke,ntokee@miitbeian.gov.cn,Female,45.148.234.27
16,Yorke,Clappison,yclappisonf@state.gov,Male,96.16.48.58
17,Cory,Mazzilli,cmazzillig@surveymonkey.com,Female,183.194.71.189
18,Elwira,aManger,eamangerh@netvibes.com,Female,191.224.20.189
19,Nat,Tomankiewicz,ntomankiewiczi@blog.com,Female,209.13.217.183
20,Travus,Libermore,tlibermorej@uiuc.edu,Male,41.195.141.140
21,Kassey,Pinkney,kpinkneyk@aol.com,Female,70.40.122.214
22,Addie,Bartlosz,abartloszl@cnn.com,Male,56.213.242.159
23,Bearnard,Elsegood,belsegoodm@sogou.com,Male,215.181.24.209
24,Drucy,Plumbridge,dplumbridgen@cnn.com,Female,122.42.217.154
25,Everett,Behne,ebehneo@vk.com,Male,171.160.25.151
26,Evelyn,Briscoe,ebriscoep@scribd.com,Male,72.86.253.203
27,Jackie,Simon,jsimonq@edublogs.org,Female,149.19.84.204
28,Aldon,Dowse,adowser@i2i.jp,Male,140.11.105.68
29,Shirlene,Medley,smedleys@engadget.com,Female,211.249.30.169
30,Evonne,Piatkowski,epiatkowskit@google.it,Female,251.215.131.151
31,Ellen,Thumim,ethumimu@wunderground.com,Female,86.26.120.17
32,Halley,Idenden,hidendenv@stanford.edu,Female,45.45.11.146
33,Yulma,Goodlett,ygoodlettw@last.fm,Male,122.93.56.34
34,Micheil,Frawley,mfrawleyx@purevolume.com,Male,5.54.31.90
35,Avery,Smallpeice,asmallpeicey@pagesperso-orange.fr,Male,65.118.105.77
36,Ermanno,McCrudden,emccruddenz@bloglovin.com,Male,58.126.246.64
37,Garrard,Slaughter,gslaughter10@naver.com,Male,20.56.57.187
38,Zsazsa,Franzonello,zfranzonello11@zimbio.com,Female,153.213.6.72
39,Salvidor,Smullen,ssmullen12@wired.com,Male,40.232.0.81
40,Enrique,Woollends,ewoollends13@bbc.co.uk,Male,138.212.197.5
41,Osgood,Hollindale,ohollindale14@smh.com.au,Male,198.207.55.83
42,Schuyler,Shalliker,sshalliker15@dailymail.co.uk,Male,46.1.187.252
43,Kirk,Fewless,kfewless16@examiner.com,Male,208.133.166.93
```

Figure 8.4   Dummy CSV data

In order to ingest the CSV data we will need to import the csv module using `import csv` and create a reader object.

> Practice this concept by completing Practice Exercise 8.7A: Reading a CSV File.

As you can see, we use the standard file reading `open()` function within a context manager with the read mode. We then create a reader object to help us read the CSV. The reader object returns each row as a list of strings.

The first five lines of the output should look like **Snippet 8.71**.

Snippet 8.71

```
['1', 'Floris', 'Reuven', 'freuven0@zdnet.com', 'Female', '217.240.50.206']
['2', 'Randall', 'Kulvear', 'rkulvear1@cbslocal.com', 'Male',
'34.22.91.187']
['3', 'Catha', 'Ladell', 'cladell2@soup.io', 'Female', '189.132.194.151']
['4', 'Orson', 'Vicarey', 'ovicarey3@mashable.com', 'Male',
'101.17.139.15']
['5', 'Analise', 'Symms', 'asymms4@gov.uk', 'Female', '189.62.145.112']
```

Because the first row contains field names, we can extract those from the output.

If you want to show the column names, which are on the first line, then you can delete if line_count > 1 and the output will be as **Snippet 8.72**.

Snippet 8.72

```
['id', 'first_name', 'last_name', 'email', 'gender', 'ip_address', '']
['1', 'Floris', 'Reuven', 'freuven0@zdnet.com', 'Female', '217.240.50.206']
['2', 'Randall', 'Kulvear', 'rkulvear1@cbslocal.com', 'Male', '34.22.91.187']
['3', 'Catha', 'Ladell', 'cladell2@soup.io', 'Female', '189.132.194.151']
['4', 'Orson', 'Vicarey', 'ovicarey3@mashable.com', 'Male', '101.17.139.15']
['5', 'Analise', 'Symms', 'asymms4@gov.uk', 'Female', '189.62.145.112']
```

After you have your data in the reader object, you can proceed to manipulate it as you want, just like any other list of strings.

WRITING TO THE CSV FILE

Writing to a CSV file is done by using the `writer` object. The writer object accepts a list of items to write for each row as shown in **Snippet 8.73**.

Snippet 8.73

```
import csv

with open('example.csv', 'w') as f:
    example_data_writer = csv.writer(f)

    example_data_writer.writerow(['name', 'age'])
    example_data_writer.writerow(['Steven', 25])
```

Running this code will create a file called `example.csv` with the contents shown in **Snippet 8.74**.

Snippet 8.74

```
name,age
Steven,25
```

WRITING A DICT TO THE CSV FILE

Instead of writing rows using lists, you can write dictionaries to CSV files. To do that, you would have to use a `DictWriter` object instead of the usual writer object, even though their behaviors are similar. However, you will also have to define a list of fieldnames which will specify the order in which values will be written to the file. **Snippet 8.75** shows an example.

Snippet 8.75

```
import csv

with open('people.csv', 'w') as f:
    fields = ['name', 'age']
    people_writer = csv.DictWriter(f, fieldnames=fields)

    people_writer.writeheader() # writes the fields as the first row
    people_writer.writerow({'name': 'Santa Claus', 'age': 1000})
```

This will create a file called `people.csv` with the contents shown in **Snippet 8.76**.

Snippet 8.76

```
name,age
Santa Claus,1000
```

Practice this concept by completing Practice Exercise 8.7B: Write a dict to CSV.

Test yourself on this concept by completing Lab Activity 8.7: Working with Files.

Lesson 8.7.2 Working with JSON Data

JSON stands for **JavaScript Object Notation**. It is a data format that was built for exchanging data in a human-readable way. Most APIs you will interact with on the Internet today will be using JSON as the data-exchange format. It is, therefore, important that we talk about it a little before we move on.

Python includes a **json** module with a few functions to assist in parsing JSON and converting some Python objects, for example, dictionaries, into JSON objects.

There are two critical methods from the **json** module that you need to know about to use JSON in Python:

JSON.DUMPS()

The `json.dumps()` method is used for JSON encoding, for example, converting dictionaries into JSON objects.

Snippet 8.81 gives an example.

Snippet 8.81

```
import json

sample = {
    "name": "Bert Bertie",
    "age": 24
}

sample_json = json.dumps(sample)
print(sample_json)
print(type(sample_json))
```

This code defines a dictionary called `sample` and then encodes it to JSON using `json.dumps()`. The dumps method will return a JSON string of the object. The output is shown in **Snippet 8.82**.

Snippet 8.82

```
'{"name": "Bert Bertie", "age": 24}'
<class 'str'>
```

You can see from the output in Snippet 8.82 that the sample `dict` was encoded into a `string` JSON object.

JSON.LOADS()

If you want to decode the JSON object, you can use `json.loads()` to do so. We are going to add some code to our original code from Snippet 8.81 to illustrate this, as shown in **Snippet 8.83**.

Snippet 8.83

```
original_sample = json.loads(sample_json)
print(original_sample)
print(type(original_sample))
```

Snippet 8.84 will output the additional lines shown in Snippet 8.83.

Snippet 8.84

```
{'name': 'Bert Bertie', 'age': 24}
<class 'dict'>
```

As you can see, the `json.loads()` function directly reverses what the `json.dumps()` function does – or rather, it creates Python objects out of JSON objects.

Practice this concept by completing Practice Exercise 8.7C: Working with JSON.

SUMMARY

Congratulations! You now have a good understanding of Python modules and packages and how they function in Python. You can now use the structuring methods you have learned to build even larger applications.

Large frameworks written in Python, such as Django and Flask, use the same principles of modules and packages that you have learned here. For reference, check out the Flask project source code on GitHub to see how files are arranged in a real-life project. You will notice that the same concepts that you just learned about are in use.

As we said in the introduction, working with data in files is a fact of any developer's life. Python, as a general-purpose scripting language, comes with a lot of built-in tools to help you read, manipulate, and write to files very easily in your program. You should now have a good grasp of how to use these tools to not only manipulate text files but also to work with more complex data such as CSV files. In our final lab activity, you had the chance to put those skills to good use by calculating wages for the employees of a fictional company.

In our next, and final module, **Module 9: Error Handling**, we will cover error handling in detail. We will also look at the built-in exception classes and create our own custom exceptions.

ERROR HANDLING

MODULE OBJECTIVES

BY THE END OF THIS MODULE, YOU WILL BE ABLE TO:

1. Describe what errors and exceptions are
2. Handle errors and exceptions when they occur
3. Define and use your own custom exceptions

INTRODUCTION

This module describes error handling in Python. We look at the try...except clause and its modified types. Lastly, we cover custom exceptions.

In life, things sometimes do not go according to plan. You may find, for example, that you have budgeted to buy certain things, but when you actually arrive at the store, you see some items that are not on your list are on sale and you buy them! That is an incident in which the initial plan was not executed well and did not produce the expected results.

A similar scenario can arise while programming. When you write some code and run it, unexpected situations can occur, which may cause the code not to be executed correctly or not produce the expected results. For example, there could be a problem with syntax, an undefined variable you are trying to use, or even a completely unforeseen scenario. When code does not execute as intended, we say that an error has occurred.

Some errors can be logical errors. These can occur when specifications are not followed. For example, a function that is supposed to return the sum of two numbers but actually returns the product would have a logical error. This is not the kind of error we will be tackling in this module. Instead, we will focus more on the runtime errors you are likely to see when the Python interpreter encounters problems during code execution.

By now, you will have probably encountered many errors while coding in Python. This module aims to equip you with a better understanding of why errors occur and what to do about them when they do. This helps prevent scenarios where, for example, an error occurs on your application and because it is not handled well, brings the whole application down.

LESSON 9.1 ERRORS AND EXCEPTIONS IN PYTHON

You may have noticed that we mention both errors and exceptions and use them in an almost interchangeable way. Why is that? Are they the same thing? Usually, they are. But in Python there are some slight differences in the meanings of the two words.

Exceptions are errors that occur when your program is running, while **errors**, for example, syntax errors, occur before program execution happens.

Lesson 9.1.1 How to Raise Exceptions

You can raise exceptions yourself for one reason or another by using the `raise` keyword. You will want to raise exceptions when something occurs and you want to inform users of your app, for example, that the input given is incorrect. See the example in **Snippet 9.1**.

Snippet 9.1

```
def raise_an_error(error):
    raise error

raise_an_error(ValueError)
```

In our example shown in **Snippet 9.1**, we define a function called `raise_an_error()`, which takes the error class name and raises it. We then try out the code by calling it with the built-in `ValueError` exception class.

If all goes well, you should see an output similar to that shown in **Snippet 9.2** when running the script.

Snippet 9.2

```
Traceback (most recent call last):
  File " error_test.py ", line 4, in <module>
    raise_an_error(ValueError)
  File " error_test.py ", line 2, in raise_an_error
    raise error
ValueError
```

Practice this concept by completing Practice Exercise 9.1A: Raise an Exception.

Practice this concept by completing Practice Exercise 9.1B: Raise an Exception with the raise Keyword.

LESSON 9.2 BUILT-IN EXCEPTIONS

Python ships with many built-in exception classes to cover a lot of error situations so that you do not have to define your own. These classes are divided into Base error classes, from which other error classes are defined, and Concrete error classes, which define the exceptions you are more likely to see from time to time.

We shall cover more on the Exception base class and its uses later in this module. For now, let's take a look at some common error and exception classes and understand what they mean.

Lesson 9.2.1 SyntaxError

A SyntaxError is very common, especially if you are new to Python. It occurs when you type a line of code which the Python interpreter is unable to parse.

An example is shown in **Snippet 9.13**.

Snippet 9.13

```
def raise_an_error(error)
    raise error

raise_an_error(ValueError)
```

In this implementation of our previous raise_an_error() method, we made a deliberate syntax error. Can you guess what it is?

Running the script shown in Snippet 9.13 will output the messages shown in **Snippet 9.14**.

Snippet 9.14

```
  File " error_test.py ", line 1
    def raise_an_error(error)
                             ^
SyntaxError: invalid syntax
```

You can see that a SyntaxError was raised with the message invalid syntax. You can also see from the stack trace the exact line the error occurred on and a small ^ pointing to the source of the error, in this case, the omission of : in the function signature. Adding it will enable the interpreter to parse the line successfully and move on with execution.

Lesson 9.2.2 ImportError

An ImportError occurs when an import cannot be resolved.

For example, importing a non-existent module will raise a ModuleNotFoundError, that is a subclass of the ImportError class. An example of this is shown in **Snippet 9.15**.

Snippet 9.15

```
>>> import nonexistentmodule

Traceback (most recent call last):
  File "<stdin>", line 1, in <module>
ModuleNotFoundError: No module named 'nonexistentmodule'
```

Lesson 9.2.3 KeyError

A `KeyError` occurs when a dictionary key is not found while trying to access it. An example is shown in **Snippet 9.16**.

Snippet 9.16

```
person = {
    "name": "Rich Brown",
    "age": 56
}

print(person["gender"])
```

The `person` dictionary defined here has only two keys: `name` and `age`. Attempting to read a key called gender raises a `KeyError` as shown in **Snippet 9.17**.

Snippet 9.17

```
Traceback (most recent call last):
  File " error_test.py ", line 6, in <module>
    print(person["gender"])
KeyError: 'gender'
```

A simple way of mitigating a `KeyError` is to use the `get` method that is defined on dictionaries, when accessing keys, which will return `None` or a custom value if the key is non-existent. **Snippet 9.18** shows an example of how to use `get`.

Snippet 9.18

```
person = {
    "name": "Rich Brown",
    "age": 56
}

print(person.get("gender"))
```

This will output `None`.

Lesson 9.2.4 TypeError

A `TypeError` will occur if you attempt to do an operation on a value or object of the wrong type.

Here are a few examples.

Adding a `string` to an `int` results in the error shown in **Snippet 9.19**.

Snippet 9.19

```
>>> 8 + "string"
Traceback (most recent call last):
  File "<stdin>", line 1, in <module>

TypeError: can only concatenate str (not "int") to str
```

This also occurs when passing wrong arguments (for example, passing an integer when we expect a list as shown in **Snippet 9.20**).

Snippet 9.20

```
a = 6

for index, value in enumerate(a):
    print(value)
```

This will also result in a `TypeError` as shown in **Snippet 9.21**.

Snippet 9.21

```
Traceback (most recent call last):
  File " error_test.py ", line 3, in <module>
    for index, value in enumerate(a):
TypeError: 'int' object is not iterable
```

The error displayed means that we cannot loop over an `int` object.

Lesson 9.2.5 AttributeError

An `AttributeError` is raised when assigning or referencing an attribute fails.

Snippet 9.22 shows an example. We are going to try to call a method called `push` on a `list` object.

Snippet 9.22

```
a = [1,2,3]

a.push(4)
```

An `AttributeError` is thrown because the `list` object has no attribute called `push` as shown in **Snippet 9.23**.

Snippet 9.23

```
Traceback (most recent call last):
  File " error_test.py ", line 3, in <module>
    a.push(4)
AttributeError: 'list' object has no attribute 'push'
```

 NOTE   Remember, to add a value to the end of a list, use the `append()` method.

Lesson 9.2.6 IndexError

An `IndexError` occurs if you are trying to access an index (for example, in a list) which does not exist.

Snippet 9.24 shows an example.

Snippet 9.24

```
a = [1,2,3]

print(a[3])
```

The list, a, only has three indexes: 0, 1, and 2. Attempting to access index 3 will cause the interpreter to throw an `IndexError` as shown in **Snippet 9.25**.

Snippet 9.25

```
Traceback (most recent call last):
  File " error_test.py ", line 3, in <module>
    print(a[3])
IndexError: list index out of range
```

Lesson 9.2.7 NameError

A `NameError` occurs when a specified name cannot be found either locally or globally. This usually happens because the name or variable is not defined.

For example, printing any undefined variable should throw a `NameError` as shown in **Snippet 9.26**.

Snippet 9.26

```
>>> print(age)

Traceback (most recent call last):
  File "<stdin>", line 1, in <module>
NameError: name 'age' is not defined
```

Lesson 9.2.8 FileNotFoundError

The last Exception class we will cover in this lesson is the FileNotFoundError. This error is raised if a file you are attempting to read or write is not found.

Snippet 9.27 shows an example.

Snippet 9.27

```
with open('input.txt', 'r') as myinputfile:
    for line in myinputfile:
        print(line)
```

The preceding code attempts to read a file called input.txt. Because we have deliberately not created any such file on our environment, we get a FileNotFoundError as shown in **Snippet 9.28**.

Snippet 9.28

```
Traceback (most recent call last):
  File " error_test.py ", line 1, in <module>
    with open('input.txt', 'r') as myinputfile:
FileNotFoundError: [Errno 2] No such file or directory: 'input.txt'
```

Test yourself on this concept by completing Lab Activity 9.2: Identifying Error Scenarios.

LESSON 9.3 HANDLING ERRORS AND EXCEPTIONS

Handling errors and exceptions starts long before you get to running your code. Right from the planning phase, you should have contingencies in place to avoid running into errors, especially logical errors that may be harder to catch in some cases.

Practices such as **defensive programming** can help mitigate future errors in some cases.

According to Wikipedia:

Defensive programming is a form of defensive design intended to ensure the continuing function of a piece of software under unforeseen circumstances. Defensive programming practices are often used where high availability, safety, or security is needed.

Defensive programming is an approach that's used to improve software and source code, in terms of the following:

- General quality—by reducing the number of software bugs and problems.
- Making the source code comprehensible—the source code should be readable and understandable, so that it is approved in a code audit.
- Making the software behave in a predictable manner, despite unexpected inputs or user actions.

In this lesson, we aim to show you some basic error handling in Python so that the next time errors occur, they do not bring your program to a crashing halt.

Lesson 9.3.1 Implementing the try…except Block

The simplest way to handle errors is to use the try…except block. The code in the try section is executed and if an error, which is specified in the except block, is thrown, the code in the except block is executed.

After the block finishes executing, the rest of the code executes as well. This prevents errors from causing your program to crash.

Let's see an example. We are going to use the code example that we used to describe the FileNotFoundError in Lesson 9.2.8 to demonstrate the try…except block.

Snippet 9.30 shows the example we will start with.

Snippet 9.30

```
with open('input.txt', 'r') as myinputfile:
    for line in myinputfile:
      print(line)

print("Execution never gets here")
```

The output is shown in **Snippet 9.31**.

Snippet 9.31

```
Traceback (most recent call last):
  File " error_test.txt ", line 1, in <module>
    with open('input.txt', 'r') as myinputfile:
FileNotFoundError: [Errno 2] No such file or directory: 'input.txt'
```

As you can see, the error caused the execution to stop before the last line.

We can rewrite the same code with the FileNotFoundError handled using a try…except block as shown in **Snippet 9.32**.

Snippet 9.32

```
try:
    with open('input.txt', 'r') as myinputfile:
        for line in myinputfile:
            print(line)
except FileNotFoundError:
    print("Whoops! File does not exist.")

print("Execution will continue to here.")
```

After wrapping the code in a `try…except` block, instead of crashing, the script executes the code in the `except` block and continues to next line. The output is shown in **Snippet 9.33**.

Snippet 9.33

```
Whoops! File does not exist.
Execution will continue to here.
```

Note that the way we have written our code means that if any other exception occurs, it will not be handled and the code will still crash.

You can handle more than one exception by creating a tuple, like that shown in **Snippet 9.34**.

Snippet 9.34

```
try:
    with open('input.txt', 'r') as myinputfile:
        for line in myinputfile:
            print(line)
except (FileNotFoundError, ValueError):
    print("Whoops! File does not exist.")

print("Execution will continue to here.")
```

A better way is to handle them individually and do something different for each error you get. We can implement this as shown in **Snippet 9.35**.

Snippet 9.35

```
try:
    with open('input.txt', 'r') as myinputfile:
        for line in myinputfile:
            print(line)
except FileNotFoundError:
    print("Whoops! File does not exist.")
except ValueError:
    print("A value error occurred")
```

In our case, only the `except` clause for the `FileNotFoundError` will be executed. However, if a `ValueError` also occurs, both `except` clauses will be executed.

If you are not quite sure which exception will be thrown, you can catch the generic `Exception`, which will catch any exception that's thrown. It is a good practice to catch the generic `Exception` at the end of more specific `except` clauses and not by itself.

We can implement this as shown in **Snippet 9.36**.

Snippet 9.36

```
try:
    with open('input.txt', 'r') as myinputfile:
        for line in myinputfile:
            print(line)
except FileNotFoundError:
    print("Whoops! File does not exist.")
except ValueError:
    print("A value error occurred")
except Exception:
    print("Something unforeseen happened")

print("Execution will continue to here.")
```

However, implementing this as shown in **Snippet 9.37** is bad practice.

Snippet 9.37

```
try:
    with open('input.txt', 'r') as myinputfile:
        for line in myinputfile:
            print(line)
except Exception:
    print("Something unforeseen happened")

print("Execution will continue to here.")
```

However, both approaches are valid syntax and will work just fine.

 NOTE   Python will not allow you to catch syntax errors. These should always be fixed before your code can run at all.

Practice this concept by completing Practice Exercise 9.3A: Implement a try...except Block.

Lesson 9.3.2 Implementing the try...except...else Block

In this lesson, we will implement the try...except block with an additional else statement.

The try...except...else block is a minor modification of the traditional try...except block so that it can include an else block. The code in the else block is always executed if no error has occurred.

We can implement the try...except...else block as shown in **Snippet 9.43**.

Snippet 9.43

```python
try:
    with open('input.txt', 'r') as myinputfile:
        for line in myinputfile:
            print(line)
except FileNotFoundError:
    print("Whoops! File does not exist.")
except ValueError:
    print("A value error occurred")
except Exception:
    print("Something unforeseen happened")
else:
    print("No error because file exists")

print("Execution will continue to here.")
```

If an error is thrown, the output will be as shown in **Snippet 9.44**.

Snippet 9.44

```
Whoops! File does not exist.
Execution will continue to here.
```

The output in the case of no error being thrown will be as shown in **Snippet 9.45**.

Snippet 9.45

```
No error because file exists
Execution will continue to here.
```

 NOTE   The output shown here ignores the contents of input.txt printed by print (line) **because** it is not relevant to the try...except logic.

Practice this concept by completing Practice Exercise 9.3B: Implementing the try...except...else Block.

Lesson 9.3.3 Implementing the finally Keyword

The finally keyword defines a code block that *must* execute before the try...except block exits, irrespective of whether any exception occurred.

It is usually the last block in the try...except block after all the exception handling logic and will always be executed.

Continuing with our file reading example, the finally keyword can be implemented as shown in **Snippet 9.50**.

Snippet 9.50

```
try:
    with open('input.txt', 'r') as myinputfile:
        for line in myinputfile:
            print(line)
except FileNotFoundError:
    print("Whoops! File does not exist.")
except ValueError:
    print("A value error occurred")
except Exception:
    print("Something unforeseen happened")
finally:
    print("I will always show up")

print("Execution will continue to here.")
```

The output when the `FileNotFoundError` occurs will look like **Snippet 9.51**.

Snippet 9.51

```
Whoops! File does not exist.
I will always show up
Execution will continue to here.
```

If the file exists, the output will look like **Snippet 9.52**.

Snippet 9.52

```
I will always show up
Execution will continue to here.
```

The `finally` keyword is useful, for example, in cases where some clean-up logic needs to happen. This might be closing files, closing database connections, or releasing system resources.

Test yourself on this concept by completing Lab Activity 9.3: Handling Errors.

LESSON 9.4 CUSTOM EXCEPTIONS

Built-in exceptions cover a wide range of situations. Sometimes, however, you may need to define a custom exception to fit your specific application situation; for example, a `RecipeNotValidError` exception when a recipe is not valid in your cooking app.

In this case, Python contains the ability to add custom errors by extending the base `Exception` class.

Lesson 9.4.1 Implementing Your Own Exception Class

Exceptions should be named with names ending with the word `Error`. Let's create the `RecipeNotValidError` we talked about previously as a custom exception as shown in **Snippet 9.54**.

Snippet 9.54

```
class RecipeNotValidError(Exception):
    def __init__(self):
        self.message = "Your recipe is not valid"

try:
    raise RecipeNotValidError
except RecipeNotValidError as e:
    print(e.message)
```

The custom exception class should just contain a few attributes that will help the user get more information about what error occurred. Our sample implementation has the `message` attribute, which we have used to get details on the error message. **Snippet 9.55** shows the output you would get if you run Snippet 9.54.

Snippet 9.55

```
Your recipe is not valid
```

Practice this concept by completing Practice Exercise 9.4: Catch an Error and Raise an Exception.

Test yourself on this concept by completing Lab Activity 9.4: Creating Your Own Custom Exception Class.

SUMMARY

In this module, we talked about errors and exceptions, what they are, and how to avoid them. We looked at a few built-in errors and the scenarios that would cause them to be raised. We then moved on to handling them by using `try...except` and `finally` blocks. We also covered how to implement our own custom exceptions by using the `Exception` base class.

This should give you the ability to make your programs more robust by handling both foreseen and unforeseen issues that may arise during code execution. Handling errors should also help prevent unpleasant usability or security issues from cropping up when your code is in the wild.

This course is an introduction to the general-purpose language Python. We have covered topics such as variable names; working with functions; modules; data structures such as lists, tuples, and dictionaries; and even working with files. This course is designed to get you from beginner level to intermediate Python developer level. We hope that you have enjoyed this experience. Feel free to go back to the module activities to refresh your memory regarding what you have learned.

Printed in the USA
CPSIA information can be obtained
at www.ICGtesting.com
JSHW052305181024
71962JS00004B/25